MW00637739

# A Sorrowful Journey

By Randall L. Buchman

Defiance College Press
701 N. Clinton St.
Defiance, Ohio 43512

Printed By:
The Hubbard Company
Defiance, Ohio

ISBN 978-0-9793078-0-5
Defiance College Press
Copyright 2007

# CONTENTS

The artwork on the front cover was created by Don Secondine Jr., a citizen of the Delaware Tribe of Indians in Oklahoma and presently teaching at Haskill Indian Nations University in Lawrence, Kansas.

Randall L. Buchman is Distinguished Professor of History Emeritus of Defiance College. His undergraduate studies were at Heidelberg College in Tiffin, Ohio under the guidance of Carl G. Klopfenstein PhD. His Masters studies were at Ohio State University under Francis P. Weisenberger in the field of History. He has done additional study at Kent State University and is an ABD in History and Archaeology at Ball State University. He was on the staff of the Ohio Historical Society for two years prior to eight and a half years teaching history in Ohio schools. In January of 1964, he joined the faculty of Defiance College in Defiance, Ohio, where he taught Native American History and Archaeology. He was promoted to Vice President of Defiance College in 1976 and returned to the classroom in 1986. He has remained associated with the college since his retirement in 1996 at the request of two presidents as a Special Assistant to Institutional Advancement and the Office of the President. He has been a visiting professor at Heidelberg College, Bowling Green State University, and Bacone College in Muskogee, Oklahoma, where he taught Native American History to Native American students.

He is the author of three books: The Confluence, the story of Fort Defiance; Woods Journal, the story of the construction of Fort Meigs; and A Pictorial History of Defiance College. He served on the editorial board of Ohio History, the publication of the Ohio Historical Society. His monograph, Historic Indians of Ohio, was published by Ohio's Bicentennial Commission in 1976. He has published several articles on Indian History and Archaeology in learned journals in the mid-west. He was involved in several TV productions for WGTE-TV public television in Toledo, Ohio. He is currently one of the Ohio Humanities Council visiting lecturers and serves as Historian of the City of Defiance, Ohio.

# Foreword

Ohio's Native Americans have been the subject of a great amount of our literature. The pre-historic people of Ohio have been investigated by archaeologists for almost two hundred years. The historic Native Americans have been the subject of the frontier history of the Northwest Territory. Narratives and historical novels have had these people as the central theme for generations. Life on the frontier for the pioneer and the story of the struggle for survival of the Native American has been recounted and reevaluated in current works.

One aspect, the removal of the Native American people, has had little attention of these studies. Grant Foreman, of Oklahoma, in the 1940's gave an overview of all the eastern people. Carl Klophenstein, of Heidelberg College, in his work in 1948 focused on the Ohio people and remains the hallmark of work done by scholars.

In recent years, scholarship has opened new insight to the Native American side of the whole Ohio story. The works of Robert White, Larry Nelson, Gregory Dowd, John Sugden, R. David Edmunds, and Colin Colloway have set the stage for new ways to look at the total picture of this saga. The discovery of a journal of a participant in one of the removals makes it possible to add more insight to the removal story. The journal of John Shelby serves as a base for comparison, along with other sources, to give a more vivid picture to the removal of three groups of Native Americans.

The Native American exodus from Ohio spans the entire spectrum of their existence in Ohio. In earlier times environmental changes, inter-tribal conflict, and cultural assimilation played major roles in relocation. With the advent of the Euro-American a new type of pressure, such as the Beaver Wars; struggle for empire wars between England and France, and the American Revolution all influenced the relocation of the Native Americans on the East Coast and the then Ohio Country. The Indian Wars of the 1790's and the War of 1812 were the Indians' last major attempts to restrain the onslaught of the Euro-American into Ohio.

The government of the United States attempted to resolve the issue of land occupation through purchase and assimilation. The partial humanitarian attempts failed in almost every instance. Finally, the attitude of the frontiersman and need for revenue prevailed and forced removal became the policy. Many of the Native Americans had already made the choice to move away from the white world that was encroaching their homelands. Segments of the Shawnee, Delaware, Miami, and others had moved from Ohio prior to the first decade of the Nineteenth Century. Removal by force starts with the Treaty of Greenville in 1795, when they were removed from the lower two-thirds of what is now Ohio. By 1820, reservations were allocated to specific groups of Native Americans in Ohio. The passing of the Indian Removal Act of 1830 during Andrew Jackson's first term assured the final chapter of their existence in Ohio as tribal or group identity. The most ambitious removal venture of the Native Americans in Ohio was the combined efforts of 1832. The plan was to combine all the people into one mass migration. Eventually, only four groups were willing to treat for removal: the Ottawa at Blanchard Fork, the Ottawa of Oquanoxa's Village, the Shawnee of Wapakoneta and Hog Creek, and the Seneca/Shawnee at Lewistown. Fragments of the Ottawa on the Maumee refused to join the Blanchard Fork and Oquanoxa's people. The Wyandotte of the Sandusky River area also refused to join the people at Wapakoneta.

RANDALL L. BUCHMAN

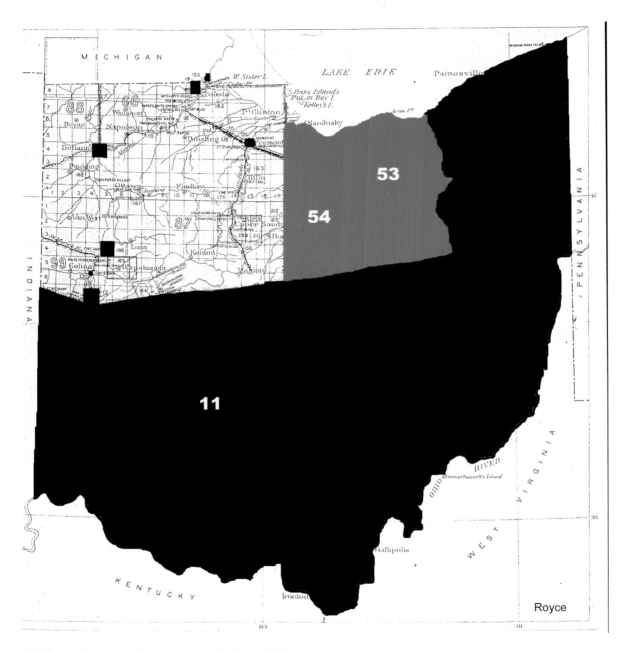

Black - Greenville Treaty
Red - Treaty of Fort Industry

# CHRONOLOGY OF INDIAN LAND CESSIONS

| Date | Location | People |
|---|---|---|
| August 3, 1795<br>* (11,12,13,14,15,18,19,20) | Greenville, Ohio<br><br>Kaskaskia | Wyandotte, Delaware, Shawnee, Ottawa, Chippewa, Potawatomie, Miami, Eel River, Wea, Kickapoo, Pianishaw, |
| July 4, 1805<br>* (53 and 54) | Fort Industry | Wyandotte, Ottawa, Chippewa, Munsee, Delaware, Shawnee, Potawatomie |
| November 17, 1806<br>* (66,169,170,183) | Detroit | Ottawa, Chippewa, Wyandotte, Potawaomie |
| November 25, 1807<br>* (70) | Brownstown | Chippewa, Ottawa, Potawatomie, Wyadotte, Shawnee |
| September 29, 1817<br>* (87,88,90,91) | Foot of the Rapids | Wyandotte, Seneca, Delaware, Shawnee, Potawatomie, Ottawa, Chippewa |
| October 6, 1818<br>* (99) | St. Mary's | Miami |
| August 3, 1929<br>* (150) | Little Sandusky | Delaware |
| February 18, 1831<br>* (163) | Washington, DC | Seneca of Sandusky River |
| July 20, 1831<br>* (164) | Lewistown | Seneca & Shawnee mixed band |
| August 8, 1831<br>* (165,166) | Wapakoneta | Shawnee at Wapakoneta and Hog Creek |
| August 30, 1831<br>* (167,168,169,170) | Miami Bay of Lake Erie | Ottawa of Ohio |
| January 19, 1832<br>* (171) | McCutcheonsville | Wyandotte |
| February 18, 1833<br>* (182,183) | Maumee | Ottawa |
| April 23, 1836<br>* (211,212,213) | ? | Wyandotte |
| March 17, 1842<br>* (259) | Upper Sandusky | Wyandotte |

* Royce Number

# Preface

The act to remove the Indians from the eastern part of the United States in 1830 ended the unsettling policy of the government toward the Native American people in Ohio. The government had vacillated and blundered its way for over fifty years through treaties, periods of conflict and turmoil. The policy's underlying motive was the government's desire for the land the Native people occupied and the lack of resources to control the natives' reaction to the policies. The government attempted to separate them from the lands it wanted by treaty as it would with a foreign power. A short period of peaceful coexistence was usually followed by conflict when the Euro-Americans violated the treaty lines and moved into the Native American lands. The major conflict that ended in 1795 at the Treaty of Greenville set the stage for the policy of reservations. The government hoped by isolating them on reservations surrounded by whites and by placing Christian missionaries among them, it would assimilate the Native Americans into the Anglo-American culture. This approach destroyed the environment that the natives needed to maintain their lifestyle. They were gardeners, hunters and gatherers, and the game, as well as the natural food source, was disappearing as more and more whites populated their lands. The government was unable to curtail the activity of the land-hungry whites and abusers of the natives.

The natives' reaction to their plight was varied. Some assimilated into the white lifestyle; others stayed on the reserves and tried to live peacefully among the whites. Many migrated farther west to sustain their lifestyle. Still others remained and fought for their land and lifestyle. The Act of 1830 ended the question in the mind of the U.S. government: move the Indians west of the Mississippi out of the way of progress. This would alleviate the fears and anxieties as well as the cost of the military surveillance of the frontier. The natives had three options: stay, assimilate into the white cultures and give up being Indian; move west and retain as much of your lifestyle as possible; or move a little farther west to continue the fight for their land and lifestyle. Regardless of their choice, it was to be "a sorrowful journey."

This work is an attempt to tell the story of the removal of part of the three groups of Native Americans who were forced by the government of the United States to leave Ohio. The author is a student of Karl Klophenstein, of Heidelberg College, who in 1948 told the story of the removal of the Ohio Indians in his doctoral dissertation. Since that time, a new source of understanding the removal of this group has been uncovered. The new source records a day-to-day journal of the removal. It gives the reader a glimpse and a hint of the ordeals suffered by these people on their trek to their new home in the West. Although an agent of the United States government writes it, there are passages that relate the struggles encountered on the journey.

The tragic story of removal of the Native American people in the southern part of the United States has been told vividly by Helen Hunt Jackson and others. The Ohio story is still part of the unknown segment of this tragic episode in our history.

The Ohio people were removed in five segments starting in 1830. Three of the removals were mostly by water, and the hardships on the journey were less than those who chose the overland route. It is the story taken from the journals of the 1832 group that is the focus of this work; the 1831 removal was the first.

The journey west is only a small part of the story that must be told to grasp the entire picture of our nation's policy of removal. The emotional and spiritual impact during removal and the post-removal episodes are still to be told. It is not only a part of their story but also a part of our nation's story.

I am grateful to several people for the creation of this book. The art work and maps throughout the text are the work of Kevin Smith, a local artist and historian. Robert B. Boehm of Defiance College and John Williams of Bacone College aided in the struggle to transcribe Shelby's journal. Loraine Andrews read the manuscript and offered valuable criticism that made it possible to accomplish the intent of the book. Carolyn Gilgenbach, Lorie Rath and Michele Tinker of the Defiance College typed the manuscript. To countless Native American friends throughout our nation, who have befriended me over the years, I owe undying appreciation. To the owners of the Shelby Journal, who wanted its story told, my deepest gratitude.

Finally to my wife Marilyn who read the manuscript and tolerated the many trips for research and my temperament throughout, I dedicate this work of love.

Throughout the work, the use of original sources without alteration appears in italics.

Randall L. Buchman
Defiance, Ohio    2007

Have we learned not to repeat?

# Chapter 1 – The People

## The Shawnee

The Shawnee, like most of the people, were never united into a single nation. Their fragmentation was the result of their divisions and their frequency of movement. The divisions, Chillicothe, Mekoche, Thawikila, Piqua, and Kishpoko, were descent groups patrilineally determined. The village was the core of the division in any territorial location. (These divisions are given various translations among the authors of Shawnee culture.) The movement about eastern North America appears to have been in sub-groups rather than the whole. Several scholars believe the Shawnee are direct descendants of the pre-historic culture of the Ohio Valley called Fort Ancient. The Shawnee are all Algonquin speaking people who were in Ohio just prior to European contact and returned in the early 1700s. At the time of their return to Ohio, there were groups of Shawnee all over the region east of the Mississippi and south of the Great Lakes.

A group of Shawnee moved to Lower Shawnee Town on the Ohio River near where the Scioto flows into the Ohio. They had come from the northeast after a period of raids and battles with the Iroquois people of the Lake Ontario region. There was considerable relocation in Ohio due to white pressures in the mid 1700s. Shawnee groups appear to have split in allegiance between the French and British during this time. In the American Revolution era, segments of the Shawnee left the Ohio country. One group joined other Shawnee groups in the deep south, one group went west of the Mississippi River, and a third group went among the Creeks in the mid-south. The last group returned to southern Ohio in 1790 and many of these joined the Indian Confederation fight against the American intrusion into the land north of the Ohio River and Kentucky. The Treaty of Greenville 1795 that ended the Indian Wars forced the Shawnee to leave their land in southern Ohio. A large faction moved to the headwaters of the Auglaize River. Once again, the Shawnee broke into factions; one group joined the Shawnee west of the Mississippi, and another left and joined the Delaware in Indiana Territory. The group that settled around Wapakoneta broke into factions early in the 1800s. The group under Blackhoof stayed in the area and remained neutral during the War of 1812. The other faction followed the leadership of Tecumseh and the Prophet and sought the British to help in their resistance to the American intrusion into their lands. This group moved out of Ohio into Indiana Territory and joined the British in the War of 1812.

In the Treaty of the Maumee Rapids in 1817, the United States granted to Blackhoof and his followers a tract of land ten miles square, the center of which would be the council house at Wapaughkonnetta. In the same treaty, Piachata and others were granted the tract at Hog Creek and Quatawapee, the tract at Lewistown with the Seneca. (See map of reservations)

The Shawnee at Hog Creek and Wapakoneta had been approached by the Quakers prior to the War of 1812 to establish a mission station among them, but at the outset of the war, the Quakers left the Shawnee. In 1819, the Quakers re-established their mission station with the Shawnee. This mission remained active until their removal in 1832. The Shawnee had assimilated many of the aspects of the white culture into their lifestyle. Many had become farmers and most had adopted the white man's dress. Some had embraced the Quaker faith and were supporting a mission school. Many still clung to their hunting ways and resented the decline in the game that was evident. There were some who resisted the white man's way of farming. In their culture, the female was the farmer and the male the hunter and warrior. The majority was still Indian in spirit and there was considerable concern over the rapid encroachment onto the hunting lands.

## The Mixed Band of Seneca

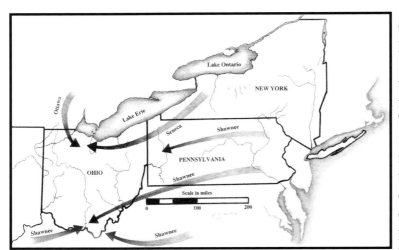

The Seneca people were the western-most group of the Iroquois Confederation in the Lake Ontario region. They were the largest of the five nation Iroquois Confederation. The Beaver Wars of the 1600s fragmented parts of the Seneca nation as well as members of the other tribes. Famine and dissatisfaction in the leadership of the Onondaga also played a part in their leaving the area. In the early 1700s, with segments of the Cayuga, they started to drift up the Genesee River Valley into the Upper Allegheny River Valley. In the mid- 1700s, many were established in the Cuyahoga River Valley near a French trading
post close to the mouth of that river. Another faction had established a village on the Ohio River under the leadership of Chief Crow by 1760. These people are often called Mingo by scholars of Ohio Native Americans. Once in Ohio, previous tribal affiliation did not have a strong hold on the villages. Iroquois and Algonquin speaking people co-mingled in villages for survival in their new locations. Segments of the Seneca joined with Shawnee, Delaware and Ottawa early in the Ohio area.

The Seneca Chief Wasp established a village in the Sandusky River Valley in the 1780s. During the American Revolution, most of these people tried to remain neutral and relocated villages away from the regions of conflict. During the Indian Wars, it appears small numbers joined the Native American resistance but played no major part in the battles. In the War of 1812, they, like many of the Ohio people, gathered in central western Ohio and eastern Indiana below the Black Swamp region. It is here that the Seneca faction joined a Shawnee group led by Quatawapea (Colonel Lewis). In the treaties signed in 1817 and 1818, most of northwestern Ohio was ceded to the United States. These treaties created two reservations for the Seneca in Ohio: A sixty-thousand-plus acre reserve on the Sandusky River and a sixty-thousand-plus acre reserve for the mixed band of Seneca and Shawnee around Lewistown near the Great Miami River (see map 2). The north one-half of the reserve was assigned to the Seneca and the south one-half to the Shawnee. The mixed band of Seneca had some Cayuga and other Iroquois in their numbers. There were around two hundred in this group.

The treaties also provided an annuity for the Seneca and others. As late as 1820, these people were living in farming villages in the spring and summer. The hunting parties would leave in the fall and hunt until December, when a winter camp was established. In the winter camp, the women and children gathered the nuts and fruits and made maple sugar. The men trapped and hunted in the immediate area. Late in March or early April, they returned to the village and started the planting of the crops. In the mid 1820s, many started to leave the village life and adopt their white neighbors' agricultural ways as independent farmers. The pressures of white settlement in Logan County and the annuity money added to their struggle for survival. The white population was exhausting the game, which was still a large part of their food source. Their annuity money became the target of white traders and whiskey sellers.

## The Ottawa

The Ottawa people are first recorded in Samuel de Champlain's report in 1615 on the east shores of Lake Huron. They are an Algonquin-speaking people who very early became involved in the fur trade with the French. They mainly occupied the regions north of Lake Huron and east of Lake Michigan. Shortly after 1700, several bands moved to Fort Detroit and mingled with bands of Huron, Chippewa, and Pottawatomie. Fragments of this group broke off prior to the French and Indian Wars of the 1750s. They frequented the area of the Maumee and Sandusky Bays and Rivers. After Pontiac's failure to drive the British out of the Lake Erie area, some joined the pro-British Indians in northern Ohio. During the American Revolution, although formally allied with the British, small factions aided the Colonial forces.

Many of the Ottawa were part of the Indian Confederation that opposed Anthony Wayne at Fallen Timbers in 1794. As a result of the Treaty of Greenville, numbers of the Ottawa removed to Michigan, Walpole Island, and Ontario. The series of treaties, Fort Industry 1805, Detroit 1807, Treaty of Maumee Rapids 1817, and St. Marys 1818, reduced the Ottawa holdings to a tract thirty-four square miles on the south side of the Maumee, a five-mile tract on the Blanchard River, and a three-mile tract on the Auglaize. The three-mile tract was around Oquanoxa's Village, and the Blanchard Forks tract was around Upper Tawa Town (present Ottawa, Ohio) (see map 2). The French, rather than the British, influenced these Ottawa to a great extent. They retained their hunting/fishing and gathering lifestyle much longer. The village was not broken up in the winter; it was the base of all the activity that sustained them. Hunting for game was more for skins and pelts rather than food. The deerskins and pelts of the fur-bearing animals were traded for much of their subsistence needs.

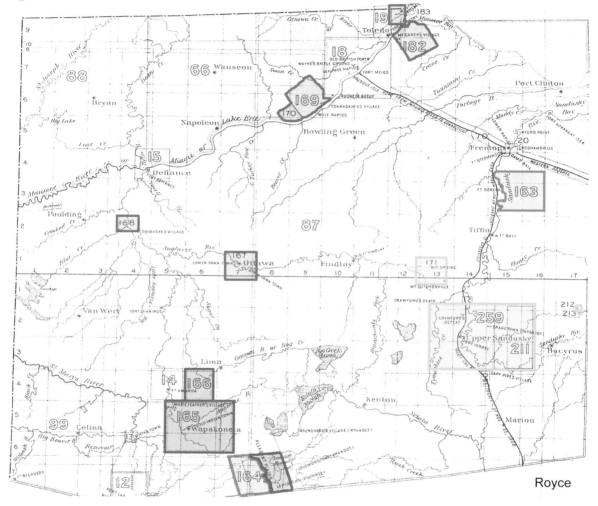

Royce

# Chapter 2 – Setting the Stage

The decade of the 1820s was a period of turmoil for the Indians who remained in Ohio. The government of the United States wanted the problem resolved but could not agree on the solution. Many of the nation's leaders wanted the Indians moved west of the Mississippi River. However, there were still those who wanted to integrate them into the white culture. The work of missionaries in Ohio was looked upon by some as the answer. There were many people in Ohio who wanted them removed because of their fear of the Indians and want of their land. There were merchants and traders who did not want them moved away. The annuities they received from the government were a dependable source of money that was the basis of their trade. The feelings among the Indians were also very diverse. Some wanted to join those who had emigrated west earlier. In several instances, those who had left returned to encourage the Ohio people to join them. Delegations traveled back and forth with a great variety of information to tell. Some said the land in the west was rich and the game plentiful. Others claimed the land was barren. Stories were told of battles between the Ohio people and the Indians of the west, especially the Osage people. Many of them went west for fear of losing their lifestyle completely if they remained among the rapidly growing white population in Ohio. Several groups of the Ohio people joined members of their tribe who lived in Indiana and Michigan, where the pressure on their lifestyle was less.

During this time, most of the Miami and Delaware left Ohio and joined Miami and Delaware people in other areas. Segments of the Shawnee and Seneca joined in this self-emigration from Ohio. The strongest desire to remove the Indians west of the Mississippi was in the southern states. Andrew Jackson, a key leader in the movement, was motivated toward removal for several reasons. He was sure it would bring security to our southern frontier. He felt as long as there was a large Indian presence, the British and Spanish would threaten our border. Jackson also felt the Indians and whites could not live together unless the Indians gave up their way of life. He felt the only way the Indians could retain their lifestyle was to be removed from the whites. Jackson, like many of the people of this period, felt using the land for hunting and food was wasteful. There was also the desire to gain profits off the abandoned land once the Indians were removed. Jackson had always felt the issue should be dealt with by Congress as well as the President. Once he became President, Indian removal became a major issue thrust upon Congress by Jackson. Once the United States government took decisive action, the Indian Removal Act of 1830, the fate of Ohio's Indian people was sealed.

*Indian Removal Act (May 28, 1830)*
*[An Act to provide for an exchange of lands with the Indians residing in any of*
*the states or territories, and for their removal west of the river Mississippi] Be it*
*enacted by the Senate and House of Representatives of the United States of America,*
*in Congress assembled, that it shall and may be lawful for the President of the*
*United States to cause so much of any territory belonging to the United States,*
*west of the river Mississippi, not included in any state or organized territory,*
*and to which the Indian title has been extinguished, as he may judge necessary, to be*
*divided into a suitable number of districts, for the reception of such tribes or nations of*
*Indians as may choose to exchange the lands where they now reside, and remove there;*
*and to cause each of said districts to be so described by natural or artificial marks, as*
*to be easily distinguished from every other.*

The government took action in regard to the Removal Act in Ohio immediately. The Seneca of the Sandusky River already had made overtures to the government to be removed west. They claimed the presence around them of the dense white population brought so many evils upon the tribe as to render its further residence in Ohio undesirable. They also declared that the game was scarce and their children were learning bad habits from the whites. The chiefs of the Seneca of Sandusky journeyed to Washington in January of 1831 to resolve the situation. A treaty was concluded with these Senecas and signed on February 28, 1831. This treaty followed the guidelines established in the Removal Act: Exchange of land in Ohio for equal amount of land west of the Mississippi River; proceeds from the sale of land to cover specific expenses of the government; government to pay for the cost of removal and cost of subsistence for one year in post-removal; and creation of an annuity. This treaty motivated the government to take steps to start negotiations with other Ohio people. James N. Gardiner, who negotiated the Seneca Treaty, was appointed Special Agent and Commissioner to the Ohio Indians for their removal. The appointment outlined instructions for the position. The Ohio Indian Agent was to be at the conclusion of all treaties. No less than equal exchange of land was to be offered, government to deduct certain costs from sale of land, and outright gift of supplies to be made, and the assumption by the government for the expenses of the removal and subsistence for one year following, estimated at thirty dollars per person.

The summer of 1831 in Ohio was a busy time for James Gardiner, Special Agent and Commissioner to the Ohio Indians. The government was ready to treat with Ohio's remaining Indians. The government thought there were about 1500 Indians on reserves in Ohio, occupying about 400,000 acres of land. Gardiner held two councils with the various groups in April and May. These were to explain the government's basic plan and to determine the level of willingness to emigrate. The reactions were mixed among the Shawnee and Seneca of Lewistown, very anti-removal among the Wyandot, and most of the Ottawa and Shawnee of Wapakoneta never showed up at these councils. Gardiner then held a third preliminary session at Wapakoneta and a final one on the Maumee for the Ottawa. He reported to Washington that there were numerous reasons for the anti-emigration factions within the various groups. The commissioner blamed the influence of the missionaries among the Wyandot and Shawnee of Wapakoneta. He also cited the influence of white traders among the various groups and the amount of mixed bloods among these people. It was his opinion that his most favorable response was from the Lewistown and Wapakoneta bands.

In July, Gardiner met with the Lewistown Shawnee/Seneca along with Ohio Indian Agent

John McElvain and the local agent John McPheron. A treaty was signed on July 20, 1831, by Gardiner, McElvain, sixteen white witnesses and thirteen chiefs of the Seneca/Shawnee. Among the witnesses were David Robb, James McPheron, John Shelby and interpreter Joseph Parks, who would all eventually be part of the emigration party. The Indians gave up their entire Ohio reserve for 60,000 acres of land west of the Mississippi contiguous to their Seneca brothers and the Cherokees. This plot of land was on the western boundary

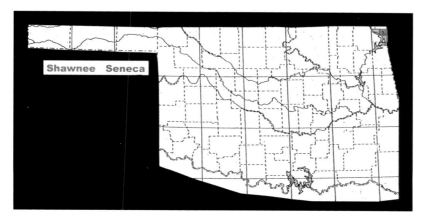

of Missouri, a part of the 67,000 acres granted to the Seneca of Sandusky. The provisions of the treaty closely followed the War Department's instructions: cession of their land in Ohio, removal, lands given to them in the west, one year's subsistence, provision for a blacksmith shop and sawmill, advancement of cash for their improvements on Ohio land, sale of chattel property, appointment of a removal agent, annuities retained, and gifts for good behavior in the past. Gardiner immediately traveled to Wapakoneta to treat with the Shawnee of Wapakoneta and Hog Creek. The treaty provisions that were presented were quite similar to those made with the Seneca/Shawnee of Lewistown. Gardiner met a more vocal resistance that he felt was stimulated by the Quaker missionary presence and because many had extensive improvements on their property. The Shawnee sought several exceptions to the standard treaty provisions. They wanted the government ot pay all their current debts in the community and grant parcels of their land to longtime white friends who were among them. On August 8, 1831, twenty-one of the various leaders signed the treaty for the Indians. David Robb, sub-agent to the Indians, Henry Walker, the Quaker Missionary, a Wyandot Chief and two Ottawa Chiefs, Tashnewau and Pentonquat, signed the treaty as witnesses. The Shawnee, in consideration of and in exchange, were given 100,000 acres of land located within the area already given to the Shawnee of Missouri in a previous treaty.

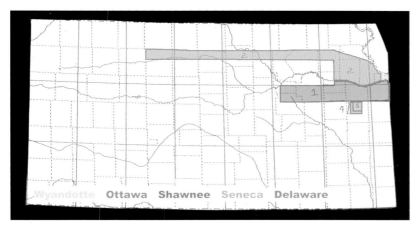

Gardiner then traveled to Tiffin and spent several futile days attempting to treat with the Wyandots before he traveled to the Ottawa at Swan Creek late in August. The negotiations with the Ottawa were very troublesome because of the white influence among the Ottawa. William Walker, a Wyandot who served as the secretary to these negotiations, claimed it was French and British influence. The Ottawa had a long association with many of the French traders who still lived and traded with them. He felt the British working out of Canada still had considerable influence over these Indians also. The Ottawa had traded with the French ever since the French arrival in the 1500s and the British were still making annual gifts to the Ottawa when they traveled to Canada. Walker suggested that the Ottawa's "deplorable addiction to intoxications" was a major factor in the negotiations. After a week of negotiating, the Ottawa agreed to a treaty giving up their Ohio tracts. However the Ottawa of Wolf Rapids and Roche de Beouf did not agree to emigrate at this time. They would remain on their land until they were ready to emigrate. They stayed eight more years before the last of them emigrated. The Blanchard's Fork and Oquanoxa's village people did agree to emigrate the next year. The treaty provisions were the same as he had negotiated with the others. Gardiner now devoted his entire attention to the Wyandots. The final resolution of the Wyandots would come a decade later after Gardiner had left the Ohio scene. John Johnston of Piqua, who had been the Ohio agent prior to Jackson's administration, would be called out of retirement to negotiate the removal of the Wyandots.

The details for removal of the three groups, the Ottawa, Shawnee/Seneca of Lewistown, and the Shawnee of Wapakoneta and Hog Creek, were talked about during the negotiations. However, several issues were not resolved until the summer of 1832. The Indians and Gardiner had thought the removal would take place in the spring so they would arrive in their new homes prior to winter weather. Gardiner was instructed by the government that the means of travel would be by Canal to Cincinnati, then by steamboat to St. Louis, and by water from there to their destinations. The approval of the treaties by the Senate was forthcoming, but the appropriations for the removal expenses were not passed until late spring of 1832. The Indians very early in the period of waiting made it clear they would not travel by water, especially steamboats.

Part of the Indians, in the expectation of a spring emigration, had sold their property the previous year. They had made purchases of guns, clothing and provisions for the trip on land. Anxiety became high with no action from the government as the time for spring planting came. The government in Washington, DC was not entirely happy with the manner of the negotiations conducted by Gardiner with the Shawnee at Wapakoneta and Hog Creek reserves. The Quakers had raised some questions to Congress about Gardiner's integrity in the negotiations. It was not until April of 1832 that the treaties were ratified and two more months before the funds for removal were appropriated.

During this time, Gardiner was arranging affairs for the process of removal with the War Department and awaiting his official appointment as Superintendent of the Removal. After his appointment, Gardiner met with each group and started the on-site preparation for the move west. The preparations continually developed new problems for Gardiner. Supplies for travel, food for the journey, securing adequate personnel, and the resistance to removal among segments in each Indian group, along with the white traders, constantly interrupted the progress. These were all compounded by the new experience of removal that was occurring in the central government several hundred miles away. It soon became apparent that another major issue had to be resolved, the mode of travel. The Natives always had in mind a land route to be followed; Gardiner's assistant in charge of travel disbursement had a different route he proposed to the Indians; and President Andrew Jackson proposed a third route, mainly by water on the Ohio and Mississippi Rivers. The fear of steam power was strong among the Indians and they were adamant in their position.

The land route presented by Gardiner's young assistant, Lt. J. F. Lane, a recent West Point graduate, was different and longer on land than the Native's route. The major objection appeared to come from the Wapakoneta and Hog Creek group. To further negotiate in regard to the mode and means of travel, Gardiner asked David Robb, whom he had asked to be Conductor of this group, to do the negotiating. Robb was ill and Gardiner sent Judge John Shelby, Robb's assistant, to meet with the chiefs in council. In his report of July 31, 1832, to Gardiner, Shelby wrote:

> They said the proposition to remove by water was not new to them. It had been made before, and they in general council had rejected it, and so informed you by letter. But at your request they had met in council again, and looked over the whole matter, and came to a well settled conclusion that they would not change their former determination they respectfully said that yourself, the Secretary of War, and their father the President must not look for them to change their opinion on the subject of removal. They further said that if the chiefs would consent to go by water, the great body of Indians would not agree to go with them; that they know the way, and would be thankful for any assistance government may choose to give them, but would go by themselves by land, in preference to going by water.
>
> The chiefs further say it as their distinct understanding at the time of the Treaty that they were to be removed in the mode agreeable to themselves. With this understanding they have agreed with the Ottaways and also with their brothers and friends of Lewistown, to remove by land. In pursuance of this arrangement they have sold off most of their heavy property, much of it at half-price, preparatory to setting out on their journey by land. They inform me they are ready to assemble on a short notice – that many of their people are suffering for food they charge their suffering to you and the Secretary of War, and say they had reason to expect they would be on their journey before this time – they earnestly request that you will furnish their poor and destitute with something to subsist on, if no others.
>
> The Indians object to parting with their horses being separated from them on any condition whatever – they say if the horses are separated from their owners they will be subject to starve, get crippled or run away for want of proper care bestowed on them. The attachment of the Indian to their horses is one heavy objection with them removing by water – they have however many other frivolous notions in regard to their health and convience, were they to go on board a steamboat, which would be tedious to me and uninteresting to you, were I to enumerate them.
>
> After reading the foregoing facts, with your knowledge of the Indian character, I trust you will indulge me in giving my opinion that it will be altogether useless to make a further attempt to prevail on them to go by water – there is but two resources left in the hand of the government, that is starvation or force. I have no doubt of some of the Indians being in a suffering condition for food at this time, and many more will soon be in like circumstances. But few of them have planted any corn, beans or potatoes: and the last years crop is nearly exhausted – game is scarce in the neighborhood where they live – when their annuities are paid, it will soon be squandered for toys and whiskey, and themselves driven to the necessity of killing the hogs, in the surrounding country or starve.
>
> I informed the Indians the money for their improvement would be paid before setting

*out on their journey – that rations would be issued two weeks before their departure from the country, and that every other treaty stipulation would be complied with in their due order and time.*

*All of which is most respectfully submitted for your consideration by*

> *Your mo. Obt. Servt.*
> *John Shelby*
> *Assist: Conductor*

Finally, on August 7, 1832, Andrew Jackson consented to the land trip as long as the cost did not exceed twenty dollars a head.

*Hermitage, August 17, '32*

*Dear John*

*Yours of the 31ults, with its enclosures on the subject of the removal of the Ohio Indians has been received. Mr. Gardiner the Superintendent can be informed that these Indians may be removed by land: provided the expense incident to such removal shall not exceed twenty dollars per head. This amount is considered sufficient for the purpose.*

*Respectfully,*

*Signed;*      *Andrew Jackson*

*John Robb Esq.*
*Act. Sec. Of War*

A squabble occurred between Gardiner and George Gibson, the Commissary-General of Subsistence in the War Department, over the size of Gardiner's staff to carry out the removal. Gardiner had submitted a plan, and staff needed with nominees for the positions as well as process for removal. Gibson reduced the staff size, but did approve the named appointees. When he later sent the name of Guy W. Pool as Assistant Agent, one of Gardiner's wife's relatives, Gibson denied the approval. Gardiner then went directly over Gibson's head to the Secretary of War and gained approval through political maneuvers. Another element in the delay was the fear of the Chiefs of small pox and cholera; it was rumored that small pox was widespread across the Mississippi River and cholera on the Great Lakes. The War Department delayed its answer of the request and funds for vaccination of the Indians for almost two months. It was late August before the basic supplies for the trip, blankets, rifles, and tent material, arrived at Wapakoneta. The delay of Congress to appropriate the funds to pay the native people their money promised for their improvements added to the impediments of the start of the journey west. The long delay situation made it possible for whites to entice among the Indians the purchase of unnecessary goods and liquor on credit, knowing large sums of money were due to the people. This money would be needed by the Indians for the trip and to start up their new life west of the Mississippi. Because of the turmoil and need to place blame on someone for all these matters, antipathy developed between Gardiner and the War Department's disbursing agent, Lt. J. F. Lane.

A portion of the Shawnee, approximately 85, refused to leave in 1832. The majority of this group was from the Hog Creek reserve and were women. They had been influenced by the Quaker efforts and did not want to travel with the main body because of their behavior. This group would migrate in 1833 under the leadership of Joseph Parks. Another small faction left from the gathering place at Hardin, and went by foot to Fort Wayne, Indiana promising to join the main body at Indianapolis. There is no record of their plight in the official records of the emigration. It is assumed they rejoined the main body along the way. Still other factions of the Shawnee refused to leave when the main body left. Later on the journey their conductor, Robb, was sent back from the gathering place to start them on their journey. This group constantly lagged behind the rest until about forty miles east of the Mississippi.

Late in August, parts of the Ottawa from Blanchard's Fork and Oquanoxa's Village started to arrive in the Wapakoneta area. The confusion continued to mount as the Natives paid their last respects to white friends and the burial sites of their family and loved ones. The plan that had been approved by the War Department was about to be put into motion. One last series of ceremonies, the Feast of the Dead, had to be done by the Shawnee. The graves of their ancestors had to be leveled and covered with sod so no trace was left behind. The celebration that followed honored the deceased members and named someone to carry on their worthy and good attributes. The plan was to start the Seneca/Shawnee of Lewistown first. They were to be under the direction of James McPherson, Conductor, and Daniel Donihue, Assistant Conductor. The Shawnee of Wapakoneta and Hog Creek were to follow some distance behind under the leadership of David Robb, Conductor, and John Shelby, Assistant Conductor. The Ottawa, led by Ben Hollister, Conductor, were to leave one day later.

The entire body was to be overseen by James B. Gardiner, Superintendent, and Guy W. Pool, Assistant Superintendent. The number of wagon masters varied with each group and each group had an interpreter. The majority of the people were mounted on their Indian ponies, others on foot or in a two-horse wagon, and a few of the elderly were allowed to ride in the government wagons. Children could ride or walk and the babies were on the backs of their mothers or older sisters. The chiefs and spiritual leaders were usually in the lead group at the start. They all were to rendezvous just north of Piqua, Ohio, at Turtle Creek, on September 18th for the start. The first to arrive were the Seneca/Shawnee of Lewistown. Fragments of the Shawnee arrived later and were joined by the Ottawa after Gardiner had sent the Assistant Superintendent to get their laggards on the move under Benjamin Hollister. The conditions of the entire body at the rendezvous were deplorable; sickness, horses on the loose and lost, deaths, and white whiskey traders turned the gathering area into turmoil. The role of the whiskey sellers, selling it by the drink, bottle, or keg, was causing not only disorder but also resistance to travel among the people. The journals, diaries, and official reports reveal the hardships and tribulations of the journey. The inability of the leader to control all segments of the emigration, the size of the group in relation to the prescribed method, and the weather, added to the situation. To the continued lack of food were added presence of whiskey, horses lost, deaths, and births during the entire journey. The disharmony between the Superintendent, Gardiner, and the Disbursement Officer, Lane, caused confusion in the route to travel and the lack of food for humans and animals alike. The story is best told by those who made it.

# Chapter 3 – A Sorrowful Journey

On July 12, 1832, John Shelby of Logan County, Ohio, was appointed "Assistant Conductor of Indians, in the emigration of the Shawnees of Wapaghkonetta and Hog Creek, who are about to leave the state of Ohio for the country assigned them, west of the state of Missouri, according to the stipulation of the treaty made by them with the United States on the 8th day of August 1831. Herewith you will receive a copy of the printed Regulations of the War Department, to which you will conform, as far as the same may be applicable to your several duties. Captain David Robb is appointed the Conductor to the Band of Detachment, to which you are attached. You will aid him in the performances of the several duties assigned him. You will obey all orders emanating from the Superintendent through him, and all his orders, consistent with the regulations of the service. You will assist in preparing a muster roll of the Shawnee tribe, and will if so required, act as a collector of Indians at the place of rendezvous. In case of the absence, illness or other inability of the conductor, you will officiate in his stead and so report to the Superintendent. It has been recommended that your pay commence from this date. And you will accordingly, from this time forward, hold yourself in continual readiness to obey any orders, relative to the performance of any duties devolving upon you by James B. Gardiner, Special Agent & Superintendent in the removal of the emigrating Indians of Ohio. John Shelby had migrated to Logan County in 1810 from Kentucky. He had served as a commander in the Ohio Militia in the War of 1812 and had witnessed several treaties with the Indians that Gardiner had negotiated. He was one of the first Associate Judges of Logan County and would spend 10 years in the Ohio Legislature. On the journey, he would be elevated to Chief Conductor of his group.

The Shelby journal for some reason was never forwarded to Washington, DC. His journal is presented parallel to the journal of Daniel W. Workman, who was appointed Conductor of the Seneca/Shawnee contingent when the original appointee, James McPherson's wife died just before departure. The Workman's journal was written by Daniel R. Dunihue, his assistant conductor. Dunihue was the nephew by marriage of James G. Gardiner and the nephew by blood of Guy W. Pool, Gardiner's assistant. There is no record of the journal of Benjamin F. Hollister, who was the conductor of the Ottawa contingent or David Robb, the conductor of the Wapakoneta and Hog Creek Shawnee. The story of the journey is based on the works of these two journals. Throughout this chapter, these journals are expanded upon by the Secretary of War to resolve the issues delaying the emigration. Daniel R. Dunihue kept a diary while on the journey and wrote to family during the journey. This diary and those letters are also used to bring a better understanding of the events of the journey. The maps that are inserted in the journals are based on the maps of S. Augustus Mitchell, "Maps of the States of Ohio, Indiana, and Illinois" of 1834. The scale is 80 miles to 3 inches. Towns, roads, and rivers are the same as on the 1834 maps. The Seneca/Shawnee of Lewistown's journey is identified as …., their encampments as ●; the Shawnee bands' journey as ----, their encampment as ■; the Ottawa's journey as xxx;  their encampment as ♦. The journals and all original sources are presented in italics and editorial comments in Times New Roman.

## Shelby's Journal with 400 Shawnee from koneta and Hog Creek Reserves

## Workman's Journal with 300 Wapa-Seneca/ Shawnee from the Lewistown Reserve

### September 18, 1832

*This morning great industry was used by our officers to put the Indians in a good state of preparation for moving to our new encampment in the Afternoon – The public waggons ware loaded with such small articles of property belonging to the Indians in destitute circumstances as they ware unable to remove themselves our camp assumed the in*

*appearance of great cordiality and industry – But when the hour was nigh for our departure – We ware informed the horses could not be found in sufficient number to attempt a removal this evening and it was a time of parting perhaps forever with many friends – Therefore they thought it would be proper to hold one more dance on the soil of that country which gave them birth and would soon know them no more forever – we received information at this time that the Indians horses could not be collected and other necessary prepertations made for a general move before Thursday morning next they gave renewed assurances that when that day arrived they would take up the line of march without further let or hindrance – This day we received separate communications from Col Gardiner by express giving instructions on various subjects and urging us to move forward with our encampment at the earliest moment possible – our officers replied seperately to the several communications though it is believed in perfect harmony – informing the Superentendant of every transaction deemed worthy of his consideration – The express is detained until tomorrow morning for the purpose of noteing any thing that may occur in the interval through the almost continually vacillating disposition of the Indians*

*A part of them attended the funeral of Mrs. McPherson who deceased yesterday, and whom the Indians have esteemed as a relative more than a friend. They say that they will start to-morrow. They were reminded of the necessity of being ready- and promised to finish their arrangements to-day, They have settled nearly all they owe*

*the neighborhood. Sixteen horses were distributed among them today.*

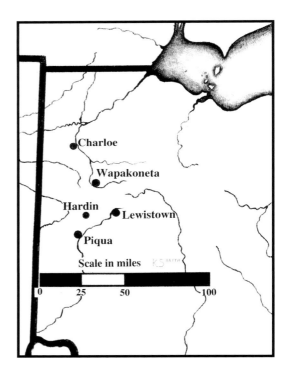

## September 19, 1832

*The express of yesterday returned
at an early hour to Col Gardiner -
with a full account of our hopes
fors and necessities – and our officers
renewed their exertions to have all things in
a state of readiness to set out on our
journey tomorrow morning  Nothing
transpired through The first part of the day
worthy of note except a carelessness and
usual inactivity in the work which created
suspision in the mind of the assistant agint
and our officers whose duty it is to watch
over Indian movements that they did not
intend to leave their present encampment on
tomorrow as hereto fore promised with
every apperance of good faith  we ware not
long left in doubt with regard to the above
suspicions – Many of the Indians openly
avowed their intention of remaining in their
present position until friday morng next – in
the after part of the day some fifteen or
twenty Indians went out to hunt and did not
return until late this evening – on this state
of things Major Pool called the chiefs
together in council and requested to know
the reasons why they had thus deceived him
by neglecting to start on their Journey
according to the late agreement which he
thought was made in cincerity – They
excused themselves by saying that they had
a religious ceremony to perform before they
left the home of their fathers which
ceremony had been performed every six
months by their ancesstry as far back as
memory could trace and they believed from
the earliest period of their existence as a
nation – and ware intirely unwilling to omit
it when they ware about to leave the land of
their nativity forever – the \*Major Stated in
impressive langira the necesitus
circumstance to which they with ourselves
would soon be for want of provisions – The
absolute necessity of removing speedily to
where it can be had – the great danger of*

*Nearly all of them left Lewistown
to-day and encamped at the distance
of 10 miles.*

\*Major Guy W. Pool, Assistant
Superintendent

*offending the \*President by their vassellateing course when he was paying large sums of money every day for their cumfort and convenience in moveing to their new homes – The chiefs replied that when their religious duty would be performed they would then be ready for their Journey and not before – that tomorrow night they would pay their devotions to the great Spirit and start next morning without fail. They expressed a willingness that our waggons containing their goods should move forward tomorrow – Thus matters stand at this time and in as much as the end of bacon and flower is fast approaching at this place we trust this fact will appirate as a strong argument in favor of a compliance with the last promise obtained from the indians than any heretofore offered*

\*President Andrew Jackson

## September 20, 1832

*this morning we ware informed
that an Indian had died in the course
miles
of the last night  This fact gave rise to
some suspicions that ceremonies of his
burial might detain us another day in this
however we ware mistaken  The Indian was
buried this afternoon  Received an express
from the Superentendant which informed us
that the Shawneys of Lewistown ware
on the march (2/3 of them) and encampt at
Stony Creek last evening he urges the
officers of this detachment in the most
pressing manner to meet him at hardin at the
earliest Moment possible.  This request will
be complied without the slightest delay on
our part for god knows our comforts are lean
enough here – We have nothing we can call
our own to eat for either man or horse  The
Indians obtained Venison to day this night
their worship will be performed things now
look fair for a start tomorrow
Three of our waggon loaded with Indian
property we look with much axiety for what*

*Those Indians who started yesterday
proceeded to Hardin, a village 19*

*from where they were encamped. The
remainer traveled 10 miles.*

*tomorrow will bring fourth About 7 o clock this evening a message was received from the chiefs stating by *H. Clay that Maj Pool – •Capt Weaver – and myself would be previlidged to see them perform their last duty to the great spirit in the land of their nativity preparatory to – or rather biding a final adue to the country which contains the bones of their parent-brothers sisters and friends and to ask his continued protection on their journey to their new home – Capt Weaver and myself attended and sat silent observers untill 11 o clock – The calm deliveration with which they proceeded in their ceremonies – The unruffled countenances over which a solemmn smile was occasionally defused – While the rain poured from heavens darkened cannopie in copeus showers attended with Thunder and lightening at intervals all went to convice us that under no cercumstance can we hope to hurry a indian to any purpose  A scene took place here Worthy of a minute discription hereafter*

*H. Clay, Nolesimo, head chief of the Shawnee
•Captain Weaver was one of the wagon drivers.

### September 21, 1832

*12 o clock – Of all the Creatures god has permitted to occupy a space on the earth an Indian is the most faithless – They can be stimulated by nothing except their animal feelings – reason seems to have no influence on their minds for the government of their conduct Starvation alone appears to be all the Mein left in the hands of the Ast agent by which he can operate on the short sighted and improvident creatures under his care to lieve this place  Day after day we have been promised by the chiefs that with the greatest apperent cencerity that they along with their people would leave Wapaghkonetta at the time of their own appointment But each day presents us with new difficulties and new excuses from the Indians for delay – at this*

*To-day those who arrived here first remained and the balance to the tribe came up at night.*

17

*moment clouds hover over our late flattering
prospects thickening as the day rouls away –
*Capt Robb sets out this moment with the
remaining waggons loaded with Indian
property •Quataway – the old War Chief
has this moment started on the journey our
prospect brighten in favor of forming a new
encampment two miles on our way this
Evening we ware informed the above named
Chief leads all great expeditians and that
now all would follow him – time will soon
prove the truth of the report    Six o clock
this evening a new encampment is formed
this evening two miles on our way
consisting of upwards of 100 our prospects
are flattering out this time that we will bid
final adue to Wapagh to morrow*

*Captain David Robb was the
Conductor of this detachment.
•Shelby's spelling of Quatawapea,
Colonel Lewis*

## September 22, 1832

*we found it impossible to remove
from our new encampment or to
collect all from our old one on accunt of
Indian tardiness    Sickness in the camp and
loss of horses    Tomorrow has often decevid
our hopes since we have been in Wapagh yet
we again trust with unusual confidence to
what it may bring fourth but few tents
remain on our old encampment
Col Gardiner arrived at Wapagh this
afternoon his presence seems to infuse new
life and new vigor in the minds of the
Indians and white men concerned in the
Immigration where ever he goes*

*By order of Col. Gardiner the Indians
remain at their encampment to-day.
Orders signed.*

## September 23, 1832

*The detachment was ordered to
march this morning. The encampment
late in the evening at the distance of
18 miles from Hardin.*

## September 24, 1832

*We struck our tents at 8 Oc. And marched to Greenville, 14 miles. We could have gone further, but a severe storm arose to prevent us.*

## September 25, 1832

*Upon a solicitation of the principal chief and others, the Indians were permitted to remain n camp long enough to dry their tents & blankets which were wet in the rain yesterday. At 11 Oc we marched on, and at sun-set encamped at the distance of 13 miles from Gr on the road toward Richmond, Ind.*

## September 26, 1832

*We struck our tents at 10 Oc and marched 10 miles being within 4 miles of Richmond, near which place we were order to remain, by the Supt until further orders should arrive from him.*

## September 27, 1832

*The Indians having an intimate acquaitance with many persons at Hardin and Its neighborhood this circumstance caused them to be tardy in their movement from this place It was near twelve oklock before they could be prevailed to leave the town   They however took up the line of march and arrived at Johnstons mill [Miami county] in the evening a distance of nine miles*

*The Indians remained at camp today.*

## September 28, 1832

*an attempt was made to start early this morning but being within two miles of the town of Piqua and a traveling shew of animals and wax figures ware*

*Nearly all the Indians went into town to-day – some to see the place, some to trade, and some to get intoxicated.*

*exhibiting at that place nothing could privent a majority of the shawney detachment from going to see it The principal chiefs instructed their subordinates to camp at stil water a distance of Eight miles from which place our officers found It impossible to prevail on them to go further although the front of the detachment arrived there at two o clock here we drew rations for the day and remained for the night*

## September 29, 1832

*This morning rain fell in heavy showers until perhaps eight o clock at which time there was the appearance of fair weather for a short time we struck our tents and moved forward on the road to Greenville Dark County early rain soon commenced falling again and continued to fall through the remainder of the day It was near dark when the detachment arrived at Greenville a distance of 15 miles where we camped for the night – This day the Couries waggon broke down and caused some delay {last evening H Clays wife delivered a fine daughter expect to remain here one day only}*

*A severe rain prevents them from leaving their encampment today.*

## September 30, 1832

*The rain of yesterday caused some delay this morning for the purpose of drying tents and other articles – several persons related to one of the principal chiefs took sick – this added to our difficulties and prevented us from getting under way at an early hour as we desired – at 10 o clock the detachment moved and traveled 13 miles to whitewater with about one third of the detachment the remainder Campt between three and four miles in the rear \*John Perry & •J Wolf are with them*

*We were order at 12 Oc by the Supdt to march on immediately. By night we succeeded in passing through Richmond and two miles further – making 6 miles.*

*\*John Perry, Lauloway, a lesser Shawnee chief*
*•John Wolf, Lawathtucker, a lesser Shawnee chief*

# October 1, 1832

Started this morning at an Early hour & traveled ten miles without any particular occurrence worthy of note Campt within three miles of the town of Richmond State of Indiana drew Rations for 350 Indians two days – here we remained through the night H Clay his family and connection came up this evening

To-day some difficulty arose among the teamsters which detained us until 11 Oc at which time we left the camp and proceeded through Centerville. Our start was so late and the road being so muddy that we traveled only 7 miles.

On October 1st Gardiner wrote to the Secretary of War

Richmond, Indn. Oct. 1st 1832

Sir;

I have the honor to inform you that the three tribes of Ohio Emigrating Indians under my charge, are now in this vicinity.

The Lewistown Detachment arrived here on Thursday last. They started on the 19th inst. leaving many loitering the rear-came seven miles to the crossing of the great Miami and encamped. Next day I took charge of them in person, and sent back the conductor & assistant to bring on the balance. On the 20th they encamped on Turtle Creek in Shelby Co. and in the course of the next day were joined by most of the band. A few went through the woods to Fort Wayne and promised to join the main body at Indianapolis. On the 29th they left Turtle Creek, and traveled by way of Greenville to Whitewater, 4 miles east of this place, where they remained in my order, until yesterday: awaiting until I could collect and organize the Shawnee and Ottaway, and bring them within half a days march of the Lewistown band. The band moved yesterday from their encampment, to a creek two miles west of this place, and started again this afternoon toward Indianapolis.

The Shawnees of Wapahkonnetta have almost exhausted our patience. They forfeited every promise, and abuse every kindness. It seems impossible to get them to make the least movement towards preparation. They were furnished with every thing promised and much more. We lent them twenty-five horses, and supplied three light two-horse wagons for baggage. They abuse the horses, ride them off to the neighboring towns; kept in a state of intoxication for several days together, until nature sunk under their beastly intemperance. During this time, I was laboriously engaged in preparing the Lewistown Band, with whom I had much trouble owing more to the intrigues and frauds of the whites among them, than to any other cause.

At length I was compelled to go back to Turtle Creek & Wapahkonnetta, myself, and send forth the Seneca under their conductor, I found the Shawnee in a most unattained situation. Many sick-some wounded-their own horses all astray-and all that could still drink whiskey women as well as men, half crazy and inebriated. I will not attempt to describe the exertion necessary to bring any thing like order out of this human chaos. I succeeded, however in getting them on by dozens to Turtle Creek-distant of 9 miles-until the main body of them, assembled and prepared for the march. The whites beset us again with their barrels and kegs of whiskey hid out in the woods and three days were consumed in almost fruitless efforts to remedy the serious evils implied by our own citizens.

*I found the Ottaway- about 100-also near Wapaghkonnetta. Many were drunk and the chiefs highly incensed at not having received their annuities. I had sent an express to Col. McElvain to meet me at Hardin, on Turtle Creek and there pay the $370 sent by Gov. Porter Of this I informed the chiefs-coaxed-flattered-scolded and threatened-and finally they followed me to Hardin-received their annuities-guns-blankets-sheeting-25 US horses-17 saddles-and two wagons to carry their baggage. Since then they have behaved as well as can be expected from them.*

*On Friday last the Shawnee and Ottawa set out on their march from Turtle Creek to this place about 60 miles-keeping a few miles apart. We had all sorts of trouble to get them this far. Fortunately, I have the confidence of all the chiefs and head-men of both bands: and when present, can govern them. The several assistants, to who they at first paid little attention (I know not what cause)-are now gaining a proper authority over them, and able to manage them in my absence. With one or two exceptions-no inexperienced men could be more efficient than the gentlemen associated with me. They are zealous, active and energetic, and fear neither weather nor hard work to facilitate my operations.*

*I hope we shall now do well. We are getting away from the old haunts and associations of the Indians. I would to God I could say we were also away from those mean and miserable retches, who, for a paltry gain, causing disorder, mutiny and dissention into our ranks, as we pass along the road, and into our camps at midnight. No human vigilance can guard against them. We have done all –every thing we could think of- to check and prevent it. The evil has abated, to be sure, since we left Greenville, in Darke Co.-but even in this moral and enlightened community-composed principally of members of the Society of Friends-wretches are found to waylay the miserable Indian with a keg or a jug-prostrate him by the road side, or in the street, and filch away his last penny! We have organized a corps of sober Indians to guard the camp and the experiment so far has proven salutary.*

*This rapid sketch is all I have been able to write you since I set out. I can truly say I have not slept three hours in any one night, for the last two weeks- and in the day time I am incessantly and most arduously engaged. I have not found it possible to take time to make out any estimates to the Commissary Gen for funds-but will do so as soon as practicable. I must keep all the three Detachments moving. We fail if we stop three days, between this and the Mississippi. I trust we shall still succeed in getting thro and realize your best wishes and expectations.*

*With great respect & esteem*

Hon. Lewis Cass,
Secry. War

*Yr. Mo. Obdt. Serv.*
*James B. Gardiner*
*Superintendent*

## October 2, 1832

*Rain began to fall early this morning – the Chiefs and Indians generally refuse to leave the present encampment until the weather should clear up  Alledgeing the impropriety of traveling in the rain with their Sick and infirm –*

*Struck our tents at 9 Oc and marched 13 ½ miles, where we halted for the night.*

*Humanity would seem to forbid the conductors from insisting on traveling this day in as much as we have eight Sick exclusive of three Squaws whose children are four six and eight days old - Rain continued to fall with Short intervals all this day and we remained in camp*

## October 3, 1832

*This morning the sun rose Clear and Seemed to offer a fair prospect of making a good days travel but we had to pass through the town of Richmond where many of our detachment got drunk and produced much delay   We campt half a mile West of Centerville having traveled a distance of only ten miles This day rcvd 240 rations bacon & 290 lb flour.*

*At 10 Oc we commenced traveling at 5 gained the distance of 15 miles.*

## October 4, 1832

*Was a day of Ill luck many of our detachment kept drunk through the last night and ware of course in a bad condition to start early this morning – The weather being fair the Conductors used every means in their power which ware likely to prevail on the detachment to move forward – But on further inquiry It was found that our sick had increased and that the child of an influentionl was expected to die this day we however set off about 9 o clock leaving about fifty behind in their tents detained either by sickness sympathy or drunkenness – The remainder of the detachment traveled four teen miles and ware compeled to make a retrograde movement of 3 miles for want of Water and pastureage and Campt one half mile west of Dublin having gained only 11 ½ miles – here water was plentiful but no pasture or forrace worth notice could be obtained – the Indian horses ware turned into the woods almost bare of vegitation*

*We commenced marching at 9 Oc and at 5 encamped at the distance of 16 miles from our last encampment.*

## October 5, 1832

*Fair weather continues  The conductors rose at break of day and started the young men to hunt horses the horses ware collected without much delay but a strong desire was manifested to wait for those who remained with the sick at the camp near Centerville  The conductors remonstrated against delay and shewed the necessity of traveling speedily towards our next deposit of provision  The detachment moved forward and campt at Blewriver near Knights town a distance of 17 miles last night another child was born in campt being the fourth birth since we left Wapagh & yester one child died at the camp near Centerville*

*We started at 9 and passed Indianapolis, making to-day 18 miles.*

## October 6, 1832

*Last evening our Camp was incumbered at an Early hour by the white population from the neighbouring villages Knights town – West liberty - & Rays town  There was of every age form infant at breast to hoary age male and female and of every hue from white to as black as jet – Some thing similar to this had appeared at every encampment since we arrived at Hardin a little town on turtle creek waters of Big Miami but not to so great an excess Here we ware compeled to order the white population from the camp that the Indians might have room to attend to their necessary Business Rain began to fall early this morning and it was with much difficulty that chiefs ware prevailed on to break up our encampment – Major Pool promised the principal Chief if he would start a few miles we would obtain better pasturage and there wait for Wolf – Perry – Clay and others until they would over take us  The detachment then moved forward  Rain soon began to fall heavyly and continued through the day The women and children ware pitiable*

*We remained in camp to-day. Our orders from, the Superintendent were to remain near this place until he should direct us to proceed In the evening the Supdt. arrived at Indianapolis.*

24

*objects to look on – an occasional laugh and cheerful countenances among them was all the consolation their conductors received in this days Journey having advanced Sixmi we encampt for the night on the waters of blue river –* *Mr Merrit came up with us this evening – he states that he used his best exertion to brig up our rear but was unsuccessful he left them to shift for them selves – But not without offering all necessary accommodations if they would hurry forward with him The Squaws who have children born on the way seem to prosper under all the disadvantag that have fallen their lot – beyond any thing which can be conceived by a white and more fortunate population*

*Mr. Merrit, a teamster

## October 7, 1832

*This day rose fair and Major Pool being present took command of the detachment and proposed moveing forward on our Journey – Wawillappea refused positively – alledgeing that the Maj had promised at different times some delay that John Perry – W – Clay and others might overtake the front of the detachment   The chief insisted on the necessity of some delay for the purpose of drying tent and clothing finding that nothing better could be done we endeavoured to make a Virtue of necessity received the promise of the Chief to start early tomorrow morning and agreed to remain in camp this day – *Mr Meridith informed us that John Perry is but six miles behind us and Capt Robb  a short distance in the rear of him*

*We received orders this morning to march a few miles. The Ottawa detachment is but a few miles in our rear. At 2 Oc we left the encampment & marched 8 miles.*

*October 8, 1832*

*The camp was waked this morning as soon as day light appeared and directed to prepare for an early move on our journey   Some reluctance was showed by the Indians when they ware called to*

*We struck our tents at 9 and at 5 encamped at the distance of 18 miles.*

*proceed on their journey without giving time
for their friends to overtake us  We insisted
on the promise obtained from the \*principal
Chief yesterday and the detachment moved
forward Rain began to fall soon after we
ware on horseback – the Indians retained
their usual cheerfulness – and traveled
sixteen miles to buckcreek here we campt
for the night a beef ration was promised this
evening but could not be obtained   Some
murmuring was heard on this occation  - but
on receiving a promise that beaf would
certainly be Isued in the morning the
majority of them appered content and lay
down to rest at an early hour   We ware not
troubled this night with many Visitors the
waggoners having intimated that the collera
was in camp for this they received a
repromand the conductors fearing a report of
this nature might allarm the fears of the
towns on the road So much that the
detachment would be interrupted on their
passage through them  No news to day from
those in our rear*

*principal Chief, Henry Clay,
   Nolesimo

## October 9, 1832

*We received 334 pound beaf early
 this morning – hurried breakfast
and moved forward  The first Six miles of
the road was much cut with waggons this
greatly retarded our progress the country
then appeared dryer and Jently undulating to
white river we piched our tents two and one
half miles west of Indianolpolis having
made a distance of 12 ½ miles  The rear of
our detachment came up with us this
evening uttering heavy complaints on
account of hunger and other difficulties
which occurred by remaining behind.  The
conducters indulge in the hope that the slight
injury sustained will teach the delinquents
prudence in future From Richmond to
Indianolpolis is 66 ½ miles over one
continued plane surface with a few
exceptions for short distances on the*

We traveled 13 miles to-day over
a very bad road.

*margins streams  The late rains have caused
the roads to be deep muddy and slugish
traveling and our necessary exposure causes
the sick to increase in camp*

*October 10, 1832*

*Last night rained excessively
 and continued to rain moderately
 untill in the after noon of this
day – The Ellements Earth and the
devil seem to conspire against us – the
frequent rains with the unusual traveling has
deepened the roads so much that they in
some places they are almost impassible –
The devil then irritates our Indians to get
drunk and White men to furnish them with
the means of doing so – great many numbers
of our detachment went to town and got
drunk some of the principal chiefs led the
way and have not at this moment returned
425 pound Bacon 580 pounds beaf 225 lb
salt and 738 lbs flour received to day.
Deemed Sufficient for 3 days we remained
in camp with some anxiety in regard to what
tomorrow may bring fourth*

*October 11, 1832*

*This day has been fair  J Perry &
J Wolf came up with us this morning
John Perry has an influence over
the nation which has very much retarded our
movements and at this moment has a
baneful tendency in our camp such as we
find difficult to controul  Perries Ignorance
and Stubornness together with the
drunkenness which at this time prevails
prevented us from moveing untill after
11 o clock The detachment then moved
14 miles and encampt 16 miles west of
Indianapolis *Black body is left behind
hunting his horse – Clay and •Wawillippea
chief
in Indanapolis drunk*

*The Indians expressed an anxious
solicitude to-day to rest themselves and
their horses, and to dry their tents and
blankets which were wet in the storm
last night & day. Their wishes
appeared so reasonable that they were
granted the privilege of remaining.*

*The detachment marched 16 miles.
No impediment.*

*\*Blackbody, one of the Shawnee men
•Wawillippea, Shelby's spelling of
  Wiwalipea, an Orator and lesser*

27

## October 12, 1832

Here *Chawways Child died and we
witnessed a second misfortune in the
same family with the meloncolly specticle of
one nation removing an other and scarcely
giving time for them to bury their dead they
are leaving the land of their nativity with the
bones of their fathers and scattering the
bones of their children along the way to see
the friends gathering around the cold
remains of a mothers Joy and depositing
their gifts with the corpse while the silver
tears rolled down the female cheeks in
silence was a scene over which an angel
might weep and not sink in dignity   The
little corpse was placed in the earth in great
haste  The detachment then moved on 14
miles and encampt west of Stitesville at this
town we left the UNS road and took that to
green Castle – Campt at Hunters

We marched 18 miles to the
Wabash River.
*Chawway, Shelby's spelling of
Chawwee, a lesser chief

## October 13, 1832

The morning being fair our detachment
moved early nothing occurred this
day worthy of note accept the road
was some worse than usual – we passed
through Green castle seat of Justice of
Putnam received two barrels of flour in our
waggons and campt four miles west of the
town drew 400 lb beaf and remained
through the night - Deercreek and the stream
next on the way are good – traveled 14 miles

We were detained late in crossing the
river. For the sake of economy many
horses were made to ford the river
while most of the women and children
were taken across in boats. The river
was not low enough for it to be
considered safe fording any but men -
or those who were good riders. The
detachment marched 7 miles from the
ferry (Clinton).

## October 14, 1832

Fair weather continues our detachment
got underway early the 7 miles of road
mudy from thence to Dickrens mill
hilly and dry here we received 3 barrels
flour in our waggons at dixens mill we strike
the big Raccoon Creek this day we travel 20
miles Campt on the creek at Seybolds here
we drew 464 lb beaf and distributed rations
quataway the old War Chief was thrown

We marched into Illinois to day and to
the distance of 11 miles from our last
encampment.

*from his horse and received considerable
injury this man and two others who became
sick ware put into waggons*

## October 15, 1832

*Rose early and started on our Journey
with great cheerfulness passed through
a delightful country  crossed the
Wabash at the town of Clinton in Vermillion
County traveled 7 miles West of Clinton to
near the Indiana line in-campt on bruets
Creek so late in the evening that it became
dark before the rear came up Indians much
displeased on accout of having no enclosure
for horses – many drunk quarrel violently
with capt Weaver and Myself – Complain of
*Jackson and Col Gardiner Threaten of
turning horses into cornfield at that they
Will reamin in camp three day - travel 17
miles and received 435 lbs of beaf*

*We started this morning about 7 oc and
marched until dark, at a pretty rapid
gait, which took us to the distance of
27 miles. There was no water to be had
between these two encampments, and
the Indians were apprised the previous
evening of this fact, and ordered to be
prepared to start very early, that we
might reach the Ambraise river.*

*Jackson, John Jackson, a lesser chief
 of the Lewistown Shawnee

## October 16, 1832

*The morning being fair   we set out on our
Journey as Early as usual nothing worthy
of note occurred this day accept we ware
compelled to encamp at the end of  12 miles
in as much neither Watter or pasture could
be obtained within a reasonable distance
We entered the grand parara this day and
traveled over a butiful and fertile contry –
Received 330 lb beaf*

*At the request of the chiefs and by
permission of Col. Gardiner the Supt.
the detachment remained in the
encampment today, for the purpose
of refreshing themselves.*

## October 17, 1832

*This morning being cloudy and misting
rain the Indian ware slow in preparing
to move and exhibited some signs of a
disposition to remain in camp through
the day having no enclosure for
the Indian horses much time was spent in
hunting them at between ten and eleven
o clock our detachment moved
forward through a beautiful parara country –
traveled 21 ½ miles and arrived at our*

*We started about 11 oc and march
7 miles to where we encamped. There
is no water for 12 miles further.*

*camping ground between sundown and
dark – watter scarce and Indians much
dissatisfied – firewood and watter scarce for
cooking supper - H Clay & other threaten to
controul our further movements – rained this
afternoon – wet and cold with out Supper*

## October 18, 1832

*The rain last evening left us in a
very unpleasant condition for
encamping at so late an hour where
firewood or watter could not be obtained in
sufficient quantities to answer our purposes
for cooking of course many passed the night
hungry and thirsty – We had no rain through
the night – drew 226 lbs of beaf this
morning – Blest with appearance of a fair
day cheerfulness again smile on our camp
and the detachment resumed our Journey
with a promise of resting at kekapoocreek
a distance of 10 miles at which place
something more than half the detachment
arrived at a reasonable hour and piched
their tent near Col Fleneirs – the remainder
missed  their way under the Direction of
\*Mj P and encampt 1 ½ miles from us
We drew 353 lb beaf and distributed 226 lb flour*

*One of the chiefs lost some of his
horses which detained us until 11 oc
when we left the encampment. In the
evening we encamped at the distance
of 12 miles.*

\*Mj P, Major Guy W. Pool

## October 19, 1832

*Fair weather we remained in camp
washed cloathing drew 370 lb beaf
156 lbs flour and prepared for an
early move tomorrow morning*

*We marched 21 miles – having traveled
late.*

## October 20, 1832

*Rain began to fall Early last
evening and rained heavyly through the
night The Chiefs refuse to move this
morning aledgeing that 4 horses ware lost
and their tents and other property wet This
was a first rate Indian excuse for delay rain
continued to fall through the day and we
remained in camp – This day an attempt was*

*This day early it commenced raining
and continued till noon, at which time
all the tents were wet, and the horses
were in the woods. We remained at
the camp.*

*made by the assistance of a half interpader
to assertain our number in camp and find
only 263 there is some mistake here they eat
the rations of 300 soldiers - 8 person are sick
and many drunk – Abram Flsnier is the
Jentlemans name where we encampt*

## October 21, 1832

*Left our encampment on kekapoo
early this morning within one and
one half miles of which we enter on a
beautiful parra 10 miles in width and in
length immeasurable by sight – rich soil and
even surface in many places as far as the eye
can distinguish appears to be sufficiently
drained – this day we traveled 12 miles and
encampt on and near the head of the little
Wabash at the farm of Mr Sawyer – neither
flour or meal could be obtained – we ware
therefore under the necisity of purchasing 10
bushils of potatoes and 130 pumpkins
for Supper – this fare received without
complaint – \*Doughertys waggon houns
broke – fastened with a chain and moved
forward drew 417 lbs beaf*

*We struck our tents at 11 and marched
14 miles.*

\*Doughertys was one of the many
  mixed blood Shawnee

### *Gardiner's Letter of October 21st to Secretary of War*

*Vandalia, Ill. Oct. 21st 1832*

Sir:

*After a ride of thirty miles through the rain, I arrived here this evening; and finding that
the weekly mail from this place eastward started this morning; I embrace the opportunity
afforded me by a traveler who leaves here for Louisville, Ky. early in the morning to drop
you a hasty line.
I left the advance detachment of Ohio Indians at Shelbyville, forty miles NE of here, yesterday morning. The other Detachments were about fifteen miles apart, in the rear – all doing
well. The weather has been much against us, and many children, and some women have
been taken sick in consequence, and are carried in the wagons. But the emigrants, generally are healthy, and in good spirits, and at length, have become for the most part, temperate.
We did not get fairly started from our rendezvous, near Piqua, Ohio, until the 27th Sept. We
entered Indiana on the 1st of this month and could, if we would cross the Mississippi before
the 1st of November.
I was compelled to haul flour from Dixon's Mill 18 miles east of the Wabash, to within 40*

miles of this place, and yet the whole expense was less than $4 per cwt. We are now out of bread entirely. Neither flour nor meal can be had, and the corn is not yet fit to hull. We are living as we can on pumpkins and potatoes as substituted. The Indians are contented, and not a complaint is heard among them. We have about 800 souls in all – a great portion women and children.

Lieut. Lane has not been seen nor heard of since Indianapolis. He went from thence to Cincinnati to procure money. He says his funds were exhausted at Richmond, near the line of Ohio. Since that time, we have been living on money borrowed from the Indians themselves and a little from some individuals among us whose private funds, brought with them from home were not quite expended. Not one of my assistants have received a dollar since we started. Still we are all doing well enough and determined the emigration shall not stop. I trust you will see by the progress we have made, that we have not been idle, nor forgetful of your instructions, to let no circumstances prevent us from arriving at our destination.

The public horses are very weak, and some of them have entirely failed. Still, we are trying to keep them along, as well as such poor and diseased animals can be supported.

Since I left Indianapolis, all our provisions have been furnished in bulk – that is, beef on foot and flour by the barrel and they have not cost us half as much, as when Lt. Lane supplied us with rations. I think we are daily living within the muster rolls by at least one third of the stated allowance.

We have fearful accounts of the prevalence of the Cholera at St. Louis. Col. Greenup, the Superintendent of the National Road, has just arrived from that city, and informs me that from Sunday to Tuesday last, eighteen deaths, by the epidemic, had taken place. I came here to-day ahead of the emigration, for the purpose of ascertaining the facts, and sending an express to Gen. Clark, asking advice and further information. Also to employ an experienced physician to accompany us, until we are out of danger. I think we shall cross the river at Alten, twenty miles above St. Louis. When I arrived here I was in hopes to find in the Post Office some further instructions from you on that, and other subjects. But I have not heard a word from you, nor Gen. Gibson, since the 17th September.

In the absence of instructions from the Department, I shall be governed by advice and opinions of Gen. Clark, as to my future movements. And I hope this may meet your approbation.

I have the honor to be,
With very great respect,
Yr, mo. Obt. Servt.
James B. Gardiner

## October 22, 1832

Weather fair The Indians being informed that we have 21 miles to travel this day intirely in parara and with out water – used great industry in cooking breakfast preparatory to starting early – the detachment soon dressed their pumpkins and potatoes and moved forward with apparent cheerfulness through beautiful planes so

We started at 9 oc and traveled late. We made the distance of 20 miles.

*extensive that earth and sky seemed to imbrace each other without hill or timber to obstruct the sight – traveled 21 miles to Kaskakei river – near Shelbybille drew 200 lb flour – dispointed in getting beaf – took a scanty suppy - have nothing for Indian horse Deep revenes near the river and poor land*

## October 23, 1832

*Camp near Shelbyville the camp was all in motiin before daylight prepareing breakfast the weather continueing fair a general unity seemed to prevail for Starting early Soon after daylight we received 452 lbs beaf and our prospects seemed to bid fair for a good days travel it was not untill our breakfast was in good state of forwardness that we learned that John Perry could not find two of his horses This circumstance caused considerable delay he at length consented that the detachment might move forward himself with the family of John Wolf remained behind We traveled 17 miles Much of the way through beautiful and widely extended pararais but of inferior quality of soil to any we have Seen since entering the grand parara grand situations may be selected here which remain open for entry the contry west of Shelbyville is but partially setle as far as we travel to day*
*Lewis Daughherty with others to the amount of 100 did not arrive in camp this evening*

*We traveled 17 miles today. The roads were good and the day fair. We encamped 6 miles W. of Vandallia, Illinois.*

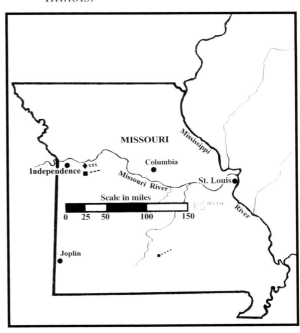

*Lewis Daughherty, another of the mixed-blood Shawnee

## October 24, 1832

*The morning being fair and pleasant the Indians ware directed to get ready to start at the usual hour we ware then informed that Perry had not found his horses and that an express from him had directed Wawellipee the Principal Chief in camp not to move under any consideration untill he should overtake the detachment*

*We traveled 19 miles. We had an excellent road.*

33

*The Indians ware informed that the public waggons must proceed together with the public horses   They remonsterated warmly against such an order.  Major Pool having started early this morning to provide food and forage  4 miles a head an express was amediately dispatched after him with a letter advising him of the existing state of things The Indians ware again called on to move forward or the public waggons and horses would leave them amediately  They stubbornly refused and commenced unloading the public waggons and tendering public horses to Mr Allen the Waggon master at this period there appeared no alternative but to go alone or countermand the order for marching   We again made a Virtue of necessity and declared we would not leave our friends destitute if they would not go with us – What influence this Vasselateing course may have with the Indians is hard to say – they are now convinced they can control our movements *Col Eberts from Washington arrived in camp last evening he Informs us that he is cloathed with full powers which may exist in the present Immigration by removing form office all concerned which he may find incompetent or negligent in the discharge of the duties of their Station – Maj Pool was soon overtaken by our express and returned to camp drew 300 lbs beaf this morning flour and meal could not be obtained and forage only in small quantities*

*\*Col Eberts, Col. J. J. Abert, Special Commissioner of the Emigration*

## October 25, 1832

*fair weather  The Indians being informed this morning that Perry and Wolf ware only four miles in our rear Consented to start early and travel fourteen miles the encamp untill Perry with his delinquent party would come up   I was directed by Maj Pool to return and assist them if necessary   I left our encampment a little after sunrise  Met capt Robb about six*

*By order of the superintendent the detachment remained stationary. An express was sent by him to St. Louis for information respecting prevalence of Cholera – the best place and manner in crossing the Mississippi river. He addressed these inquiries to Gen. Clark.*

34

*mile from our Camp and met Pery and Wolf
about 9 miles on my return found capt Robb
at Prentices tavern 5 miles from the Indian
encampment  We persued our Journey
westward to becks Creek where we found
fine pasture in the woods and doubting the
propriety of proceeding further lest should
not obtain watter we encamped for the night
3 miles from the encampment at Miressle
our meat 40 ½ lb Venison   We traveled
through beautiful pararas surrounded with
good timber the land poor and appears to
wet for to be cultivated pleasantly*

### Gardiner Letter to General Clark in St. Louis

*Hickory Grove, Bond Co. Illinois*
                    *Oct. 25th 1832*


Dear Sir,


   I have the honor to inform you that I am thus far on my way from the state of Ohio, to
the country west of Missouri and Arkansas with about eight hundred emigrating Indians
being bands of three distinct tribes: the Seneca, Shawnees, and Ottawas; and marched in
three Detachments. The first Detachment, composed of about two thirds Senecas, and one
third Shawnee commonly called the "Lewistown Indians" about 250 in number, are now
encamped on the east fork of Shoal Creek two and a half miles east of this place.
   The Ottawas, about one hundred souls, will probably arrive in this vicinity to-day.
   The Shawnee of Wapaghkonnetta and Hog Creek-so called- consisting of about four hundred and fifty souls will be up by tomorrow or next day.
   In consequence of the want of the necessary preparations on the part of the Government
we were not able to start from the general rondezous in Shelby Co. Ohio until the 27th,
ultimo. Our march, since that time has been constant and as expeditious as the weather, the
roads, and the health of the Indians would possible admit.
   With very few exceptions the Indians are on horseback and in their own wagons and
carriages. We have seventy five public horses and ten public wagons to assist in the transportation of the baggage and conveyance of the aged, sick, decrepid. The Indians are
generally healthy; and so far are contented and pleased with the prospect of reaching their
new homes before the severity of winter shall arrest their march. Many of them, it is true,
has caused us much embarrassment and delay, in consequence of excessive intemperance
which, while passing through the peoples settlements, we found it impossible to prevent. Of
late however, we have not been much annoyed from this prolific source of evil.

*We have as yet received but ten thousand dollars: which sum according to the report of the Disbursing Agent, was nearly exhausted in the preparatory measures, before we left western line of Ohio. This gentleman left us at Indianapolis for Cincinnati, for the avowed purpose of procuring funds, and has not been heard of since.*

*From the time of leaving Indianapolis up to the present period we have subsisted ourselves the Indians and about six hundred horses principally on funds borrowed from the Indians themselves! Still we have managed so as to prevent any real want, or any delay in our operations. A great proportion of the immigrants – at least one half – consist of women and children. Several of the former are very aged and inform: and many of the latter helpless infants. A few deaths from Cholera infantum, bad colds, dyssentary etc. have occurred on the road. But the number of births has been at least equal to that of the deaths.*

*When we arrived at Vandalia, I confidently expected to receive some definite instructions from the War Department, relative to my future movements. I have not, however, received a solitary line from the Secretary of War, nor the Commissary General, since my departure from Ohio. The absence of those officers from the seat of Government has, I presumed, caused the delay.*

*The prevalence of the Cholera at St. Louis, with considerable violence as we learn, has induced me to halt the line of emigration in this country for three or four days, for the purpose of asking your advice and opinion as to my further progress at present. I trust you will excuse the liberty I take under the embarrassing circumstances in which I am now placed. I have already informed the Secretary that in the absence of instructions from him, I should throw myself upon you, as a safe and ready conseller. And I have further requested him to authorize you to aid and direct me, to the end of my journey, after reaching Missouri. Deeply sensible of the responsibility which devolies upon me, as the Superintendent of the Emigration of Ohio Indians: I am extremely solicitous to exercise all possible prudence and caution in preserving the lives and the health of the eight hundred defenseless human beings committed to my care. The policy of the Government is known to be humane as munificent toward these people; and as the instrument of that policy, I feel that I should be utterly without apology, if I rushed unnecessarily and unadvisedly, into the region of a terrible malady, and thus expose to possible destruction so many of the human race.*

*I therefore respectfully ask your advice and to the proper time and place and manner of crossing the Mississippi? – the route from thence, with one of the tribes, to the confluence of the Neosho and Arkansas rivers: and with the other two to the southern side of the Kansas above its junction with the Missouri? – and the best and cheapest mode of supplying subsistence and transportation on the way? Would you advise to cross the river as soon as possible? And if not, how long, and where would you think and where would you think it best to tarry? Should I not be furnished immediately with one or two experienced physician? If so, can you send me such, or recommend me who to employ? We have $200 worth of medicine, badly selected, but do not know how to use them, on important occasions. I trust we shall not long remain destitute of funds; unless the prevalence of Cholera at Cincinnati, of which we just heard, shall delay or prevent the return of Lieut. Lane, the Disbursing Agent.*

*I think it not improbable, from certain events which have occurred in the course of the emigration, that you may have already received some instructions from the Secretary of War, which may have an important bearing upon the future organization and movements. If so, will you have the kindness to inform me of the facts.*

*My regular express is now in the rear of the line, and I have no person I can depend upon who can be spared long enough to convey you this letter. I therefore send it by Mr. McConnell, the Post Master of Vandalia, who has promised to deliver it to you in person. I respectfully request that you will send me your reply, by express, as soon as possible. The Indians are becoming extremely uneasy from the exaggerated reports they have heard along the road. And it is important that their fears be quieted as far as practicable.*

*I have the honor to be,*
*With the greatest respect,*
*Yr, Mo. Obt. Servt.*

*Gen. Wm Clark*                                  *James B. Gardiner*
  *Supt. Ind. Affairs*                              *Special Agent & Superinten-*
*dent*
    *St. Louis*                                     *Emigration, Ohio Indians*

## BACK TO THE JOURNALS
### October 26, 1832

*fair weather our party rose early and set out on our Journey traveled 24 miles and overtook the front of the detachment late in the evening - this day we passed through extensive pararais of rather inferior soil inclined to be wet – drew 312 lb pork recvd 1000 lb flour Camp at Linlies*

*Removed from the road that travelers from St. Louis might not come among the Indians, for it is now understood that the Cholera is prevailing there to a considerable extent.*

### October 27, 1832

*fair weather continues  Started early and traveled briskly through some beautiful parara though not rich skirted with indifferent timber until we arrived at Greenville the Seat of Justice for Bond County here John Wolf delayed some time unnecessarily this is Wolfs usual habit to our frequent inquiry y it however for once turned out fortunate about one half mile west of the town a Squaw was taken Violently ill with a pain in the stomach (I suppose form eating to much apples and wild grapes) and was thrown into a fit apparently hysterick she was laid on a blanket saupposed to be dieing I called a Doctor who administered medicine which gave imediate relief - the Woman was put into John Wolfs Waggon and arrived happyly in camp alittle after dark having*

*The detachment remained in camp.*

*traveled a distance of 18 miles here we
unexpected found the Senaca detachment
and learned that Col Ebert the gov Agent
had Suspended Col Gardiner and *Lieutenant
Lain This Doctor Gilman Kendal refused
pay for his services to the sick woman drew
416 lb beaf*

*Lieutenant Lain, Lt. J. F. Lane,
  Disbursing Agent for the Emigration

## October 28, 1832

*This day we remained in camp and
settled our accounts the officers
received their pay up to the 31 October 1831
Recd 265 lb pork 278 lb flour oats 38 Dozen
ans
Capt Robb went to the camp neglected his
business failed to settle his account
grumbled and whined excessively*

*The Indians remained in camp.
Quietness was exhibited from every
tent. Good feeling abundantly
prevail throughout the day. The Indi-

have not for several days had an
opportunity of procuring liquor – they
consequently remain sober.*

## October 29, 1832

*fair weather continues we remain
camp *Quaskee lost two horses,
one of which belonged to United States –
made deligent search but failed to
find them – Capt Robb resigned
the office of Conductor reluctantly is
heavyly dispised by the officers for his self
conceit and inefficiency Recd 20 Doz
sheaves of oats & 208 lbs flour*

*We this day received orders to march
by Col. Abert, who assumed the future
direction of the emigration on the 27th.
We started about 10 oc and marched to
the distance of 15 miles on the road to
Kaskaskia where Gen Clark advised
the Supt to have this detachment of
Indians taken across.
*Quaskee, probably Quakquasee of the
Shawnee*

## October 30, 1832

*Notice was received last evening to move
this morning  Mr. Merideth in
company with an Indian was directed to
hunt quaskees horses quaskees
waggon was furnished with one public horse
and one from his friend and We proceeded
on our Journey with out further difficulty
through extensive pararais appearently of
better quality than any we have seen West of
Vandelia they are however believed to be a
wet coald Soil – Corn is uniformly shorter
than we have ever seen before on a soil*

*In consequences of some of the early
principle men of the tribe being behind
the Indians refused to go until they
could come up. It was not till noon that
they arrived, and it was then too late to
get to the next stream of water – so we
were compelled to remain.*

*having the appearance of so much fertility
We traveled 20 miles this day and encampt
on Silver Creek drew [no amount] lbs beaf
and 345 Sheaves oats*

### October 31, 1832

*Camp at Silvercreeek fair-weather continues
The Indians Ware urged to Move early
this morning that we might arrive incamp
early for the Special purpose of Col Ebert
holding a council with the Chiefs in
regard to crossing the Mississippi on
tomorrow & our movement in future
We ware soon under Way and
traveled briskly to Edwards Ville here
Perries Mare & Colt was sold with his
concert for 5$ as Was also a horse beloning
to a Squaw Sold for alike sum and one
given away owned by the same woman
a considerable number got drunk here
as usual in such places – a Quarrel arose
a little west of the town & Black body
wounded severely by a stroke with a gun
from *Jo Daugherty traveled through a large
pararais of beter quality than those seen
yester day – Passed through the northern
end of the American bottom – Some fine
pararai rich as heart Could Wish - Campt
at Wood Creek haveing traveled 18 miles*

*We marched 14 miles.*

*Jo Daugherty, Joseph Daugherty, a
mixed-blood of the Shawnee

### November 1, 1832

*fair weather conditions the Indians rose early
many of them extremly anxious to see the
Mississippi river – Breakfast was prepared
in haste the quarrels of last evening being
the Result of drunkenness ware apperently
forgotten And we Set out on our Journey
with great cheer Fullness and Soon arrived
at the Village of Alton From which point we
ware to cross the king of Watters in the
Western Country the day was spent in
crossing the river – Many got drunk and
spent the night on the Misoura side in noise
and rioting at a distance of Six miles from*

*A chief and his son were left behind
yesterday to hunt for their horses, and
have not yet come up. The chiefs here
refuse to leave him any further behind.
They say that they are afraid that they
are lost. We were consequently
compelled to remain for those behind.*

39

*our last encampment - no rations Isued this evening some ware hungary some drunk some mad and Some cheerful – The upper end of the American botom offers many rich and beautiful prospects this botom is supposed to be the largest on the North American continent –
Lt Lane challenges Col Gardiner*

## November 2, 1832

*fair weather continues and much drunkenness appears in camp this morning – an other child born in camp \*Chels Daungerty wife - The debach of last evening prevents an early start this morning – It was near 12 o clock before we ware able to move forward We traveled 9 miles between the two famous river Misoura & Mississippi and the point where we encampte both are to be seen here is certainly Some of the most delightitful spots under heaven – Illinoss river pours her mighty flood into Mississippi in sight of this place If human being can be healthy here It surely the choicest spot in the Western World*

*We struck our tents at 8 oc and encamped at 5, having traveled 17 miles.*

\*Chels Daungerty, probably Charles Daugherty's wife

## November 3, 1832

*Last evening a child died belonging to the family of \*Spy buck one of the Chiefs of the Shawney tribe – Preperations ware made by the Conductor for an early burial but they being unwilling that the corpse Should be intered until after 12 o clock It was perfarid to carry the corpse forward and bury tommorow Morning this was agreed to a considerable number of Indians remained behind drunk on the West bank of the river near Alton this formed a good Indian excuse for those who ware Sober to delay until their friends should come up to our encampment But after being promised a Short march they Set off on their Journey at 11 oclock with their usual cheerfulness - A hope of obtaining forrage watter and pasturage induced the assistant super intendant to incroach on his*

*We marched 14 miles.*

\*Spy buck, Saucothcaw, a lesser chief

*promise of a short march  We traveled 16 miles and encamp at Judge Spencers on a creek called Dardenell upon the road to South river – great dissatisfaction prevailed this evening on account of a long march and encampment - Judge Spencer refused his fireside for the accommodation of our officers – fearing cholera - a poor Frenchman took Capt Weaver and myself - Passed through fine land but sickly*

## November 4, 1832

*Rained a very light shower Last night and continued to mist lightly this morning – Spy bucks child was buryed early this morning - Wawillippee Lost two horses last night but concented the people might go forward under promise of a short march miles  We Started off late traveled through a high barony country destitute of water ware compelled to travel 15 miles to pond fort - many camp on the way others arrive in camp at dark great dissatisfaction prevails in camp the Indians believe a discptin was practicticed on them knowingly - cast up their former treatment in regard to long marches - We traveled to day on the high lands between Mississippi and Misoura beautiful country said to be healthy but destitute in many places of timber and water - water cannot be obtained here for diging  - many have cisterns sunk in the ground to obtained water from the Roofs of their houses - a few fine springs are sparsele scatered over the country*

*We traveled 20 miles which brought us to within 4 miles of the ferry at the Mississippi where we were to cross. The Condt. rode to Kaskaskia to see Col P. Menard, to who he was directed by Col. Abert for information of 6 or 8 respecting the route, and assistance in crossing the river. In the evening the condt. returned to camp.*

## November 5, 1832

*Camp at pond fort  Rained light showers this morning The Indians ware Very trady in their movements on account of the inclemency of the weather - It was soon assertain that 9 horses ware Missing - Many complaints are again uttered concerning our late encampmt last evening – scarcity of*

*The 5th of November is missing from the documents.*

*wood and provision roused the Indians to
industry after being promised better fare
some four miles ahead We set out in the
rain traveled 4 ½ miles and encampt on the
farm of Mr Amos - Soon after we had
pitched our tents I was informed that an
ottawwouy Indian lay by the Road side Sick
and beging for water I borrowed a caffy pot
and returned to him with water - found him
in great pain accompanied with severe
spasms - became all alarmed lest the disease
might be cholera – gave an Indian 25 cents
next morning to carry more water - the
Sufferer found alive*

### November 6, 1832

*Cloudy and cold an attempt was made to
starte early this morning but objections
ware offered from different parts of the camp
amongst which ware the loss of horses night
before last 9 in number friend behind -
This is the 3 day since I became unwell and
not being able to go through the camp as
usual – cannot give the several reasons
offered for delay – We remain in camp –
Col Abert past us to day*

*This morning the Indians proceeded
to the ferry. The wind blew so severly
that the ferryman refused to cross.
It continued all day.*

### November 7, 1832

*Cloudy and Cold The Indians leave the
camp with great reluctance Insist much
on our lantord to sell Whisky *Assistant
Conductor protem Imprudently purchase
whisky for the Chiefs - Wawillippe
Near ■Cornstalk & H Clay get drunk and
fight on the way - We pass the ottaway
Camp the chief is dead two others appear
in dieing circumstances – Doct Wright
declares the disease to be Cholera –
Blackbody a ▲ Missessinnay receive the
corpse into their waggon - Conductor of
Shawneys forbid them bringng the corpse in
his camp - they received it not with standing
- Travel 16 miles to Bevins Creek and
encamp at Mr Morgans late in the evening –*

*To-day about two-thirds of them were
taken over which occupies their time
until dark.*

*\*Assistant Conductor, Benjamin  •Mc-
Hollister
•McNear, Peaghtucker, a lesser chief
■Cornstalk, P. H. Thawataw signed the
 Treaty of Removal*

*▲ Missessinnay, Missinneway, one of
 the Shawnee*

*many complaints uttered isue meat and*
*flower plenty and good humour soon*
*prevails in camp - trave through poor contry*
*destitute of timber water and houses*

## November 8, 1832

*Cold frosty morning but many*
*appearances of a pleasant day  we set out*
*early on our Journey and traveled a high*
*contry principally parara extending in many*
*places on our right beyond our utmost*
*Streach of Sight  soil poor and washes easy*
*by rains traveled 14 miles and encampt off*
*the road near Esqr Ruliys*

*The remaining part of the Indians were*
*taken over today.*

## November 9, 1832

*It was discovered early this Morning that*
*one chesnut Sorrel horse with both hind*
*feet White the property of the U N States*
*was missing  Also one small brown mare*
*belonging to the U N States a sore on the*
*middle of her back – Indians ware imployed*
*to search for the beforementioned beasts but*
*returned unsuccessful  The detachment*
*moved forward through extensive*
*pararais - -The weather fair and not a cloud*
*to be seen accept those formed by the*
*smoke from burning pararais Those Volumns*
*of smoke ware to be seen in Various directions*
*curling their towering tops toward heaven*
*About three miles from our camp I discovered a*
*bay horse 8 years old 14 hands high and*
*branded U.S. laying by the wayside having*
*gave out under excessive fatieuge  - took*
*him to Lewiston a small Village in sight –*
*offered to Sell him for five dollars - could*
*find no purchaser - told Friderick A*
*Hamilton & Jacob L Sharp - is clark of the*
*court - to feed him until called for by some*
*one authorized - at $1.75 cts per week  We*
*traveled 15 miles to day passed intirely*
*through 20 mile parara and campt near its*
*West end at place called buterlick*

*The Indians remained at camp for*
*purpose of getting their horses shod.*

## November 10, 1832

beautiful Weather continues having fed
our horse will last night and this morning
We endeavoured to start early but on
examination it was found our sick had
some increaset and Wawwillippes
head became much inflamed after his
Drunken battle with McNear he applied to
ride in a waggon passed through a
considerable tracts of timbered Country poor
rocky and ridges - then through beautiful
pararais - arrived late in the evening at
Vausc river - obtain neither meat or
forage  - The Indians in bad humor
Our travel to day is 16 miles We are
informed to day that 4 ottaw ways
are dead - the people are much  allarmeded
for fear of Cholera - The Conductors of
ottawe ways believe fatal disease is in their
camp

The Indians had considerable difficulty
finding their horses. We started late,
and traveled only 8 miles.

## November 11, 1832

fair weather continues the detachment
Started early as usual and Soon entered a
beautiful parara Some richer than any
passed within the two last days –
this is a part or arm of the Grand
Parari West of Mississippi and is said to
extend with short intervals of timber
northward to the Rocky Mountains although
the surface of this fine parara appears in
most parts no more uneven than is necessary
for draining the Contry yet in many
directions a tree or shrub could not
be seen - Earth and Sky appears to meet
together without an obsticle to Interrupt the
sight - We encampt near the western edge of
this arm of pararai having traveled 16 miles
- To east Cedercreek  It is proper to note
here that an Iron gray horse 3 years old
belonging to U N S was found near our
camp unable to rise to his feet and believed
to be dieing from Want of sufficiend forage
and exausted by fateauge  - the horse was in

We traveled 18 miles.

### November 12, 1832

*fair weather continues - started early as
usual - passed through a poor hilly
timbered country - Passed through
the town of Columbia – trav 16 miles this
day - Campt late in the evening at a creek
called Peetwessa a squaw died in the
Public Waggon this day on the road Samuel
Burris shewed this evening the first shred of
hospitality seen in Misoura - he is Virginian
great solitude evinced and almost continual
inquiries made by travelers in regard to
Cholera in our Camp forrage scarce this
evening - agents scattered  - much
dissatisfaction prevails among the Indians
Perry and Clay threaten to apply to Col
Ebert for redress - Campt at Roche  percia
or Rockriver*

*We traveled 17 miles.*

### November 13, 1832

*fair weather continues - the corpse of
Pesitwesse ware to be buried this
morning this furnished a good Indian
ing excuse for one days delay - we
however urged the burial with a view of
starting imedialy afterward John
Perry Promised to start imedialy after the
interment But privately informed the
detachment that the camp would not move
to day – and sliped off with the scounderal
Henry Clay to the town of Columbia four
miles in our rear to complain to Col Abert of
bad treatment  I soon found that Perries
bet was immoveable from at least one half
the detachment and believing it necessary to
rest and feed the horses at least one day
wash clothing & I agreed to remain in camp
- but not without some regrets to find
myself overreached by a faithless Indian*

*We traveled 4 miles – 1 west of the
Mine of Buston, where we encamped
for the purpose of having the remain-
part of the horses shod.*

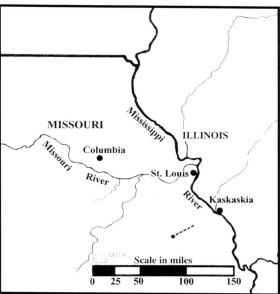

## November 14, 1832

fair weather continues we left our camp
at 11 o clock  The Indian start this morning
with great reluctance and expect
indulgeacencs from Col Abert  We
traveled about 12 miles and encampt on
small river called Moniter one mile short
of the place directed - This was done by
Wawillippee while the Conductor
was some distance in the rear sharp words
took place between the Conductor and the
Indian chief the camp became immoveable
and we remained here through the night
This days travel wis principally through a
rich contry of timbered land apparently high
and healthy but destitute in a great measure
inregard to Springs or standing water

We remained today for the purposed of
getting horses shod, and giving the
Squaws an opportunity of washing their
clothes and blankets.

## November 15, 1832

Clear Cold Weather thous but little to day –
last night M-Hardins squaw had a son this
is the 6th birth on our way Waggons much
crowded – many complaints cannot be
satisfied  We however started at 10 o clock
and traveled over a high ridge contry
covered with almost every species of timber
and shrub which grows in both rich and
poor land passed through the town of
Franklin and Campt in the Misourie botom
having traveled 11 miles – here a drunken
Indian quarreled

It was late this morning before the
Indians could collect their horses.
We traveled 8 miles.

## November 16, 1832

The weather cool dry and Clear the
detachment moved at the usual hour and
traveled on the fertile botoms of the
Misourie 12 miles to the ferry at a
point called Arrow Rock - about one half
the detachment crossed over this after noon
there being two rival ferries here our
crossing was  much expedited and our
ferriage at half price an Indian called
_____ died in the waggon to day of a

We traveled 16 miles to the Merrimack
river.

46

*lingering consumption as we passed on with out a frind present except his wife to witness his last departing moments when he was about to bid adue to time forever Arrow rock is a new Village just commencing on the south west bank of the river in Salene County this county and the ajoining Countys of Howard and Boon abounds in salt springs and stone coals salt fountains are decr*

## November 17, 1832

*The remainder of our detachment crossed over early in the day and began to prepare for burying the man who died yesterday at this time the conductor had comfortable hopes of moveing a distance of 4 miles But Maj Pool and Capt Weaver not having arrived every necessary duty to expedite our movement could not be discharged by the conductor and his assistant  The howns of J Perries Waggon broke at rising the hill near the ferry - much difficulty in finding a workman to repair it – Rain began to fall in the after part of the day and we agree to bury our dead repair our waggons and remain in camp - a cabinet maker mend Perries Waggon - We put up at the hous of Mr Brown*

*A family was left behind a day or two ago which the Indians say they intend waiting for at this place.*

## November 18, 1832

*last night rained and froze considerably – continued to rain with a mixture of Snow until 12 o clock – turned colder in the afternoon - northwest  blows heavyly – snow falls fast - We remain in camp*

*It rained all day, so much that the Indians would not start.*

## November 19, 1832

*This morning is stormy and very cold we remain in camp - the fine steam boat Chieftain arrives- Superintendant Attempt to charter her to convey the Indians to Kanzas - The Capt refuse for fear of ice*

*It was so cold that the Indians refused to travel. It snowed and blew terribly.*

*Drunkenness in camp as usual when near town - grocery keepers all unprincipaled*

## November 20, 1832

*Clear and cold this morning the river Misourie runs with ice on the surface so thick that it is impassible by water crafts – The ottaw ways are on the oppisite to the town near which the Shawney detachment are encampt The chiefs ware consulted early this morning in regard to our removal and their consent obtained The public waggons ware ordered to be in readiness soon afterwards we ware informed that John Perry had given notice to the camp not to move to day and directed the young men to go in persuit of game this information led to Some altercaton between the several agents and the principal chiefs of the tribe in which they obstinately refused to go presenting their frozen tents and the condition of their woman and children to be moved in cold weather for their Justification – The conductor with the approbation of Col Abert threatened to remove the public waggons - They replied go on give us our goods - It was at length determined to remain in camp this day and withhold forrage and provisons - The chiefs demand the rifles due them from the Gov by treaty Col Abert dilivers the guns and the chiefs Distribute It is determined move tomorrow let the result be what it may*

*A child died this morning (the only death which occurred in this tribe) which detained us until late. Some horses strayed away which added to the delay. Traveled 7 miles.*

## November 21, 1832

*Clear and cold this morning - ice much increased in the river - Snow remains on the ground - thaws but little through the day - travel through or rather in a firtile and beautiful parara as extensive as our sight with the exception of a few stunted groves interspersed over the face of the contry - Stone coal and Salt Water abounds in part of this contry - Contry better wattered*

*We traveled 18 miles.*

*than usual further eastward  The detachment traveled 8 miles this day and encampt in a small grove near Mr Smiths - The old White Woman of \*Daughherties family died here this evening before She was taken out of the Waggon - our flour waggon Fails to arrive in camp - beaf cannot be obtained Consequently no rations Isued - This morning Jo Barnet presented some receipt for expenditures while under the safe Conduct of Capt Robb to Col Abert for remuneration - he was informed that Capt robb should have setled or cirtified to their correctness - he replied that Capt Robb was seldom up with the detachment and when up that it would require the assistance of two Indians to keep him there - Mr Merit attests to a semiler fact in a letter to Major Pool couched in humourous language –*

*\*Daughherties; there were three Daugherty families on the role: Jacob, John and Lewis.*

## November 22, 1832

*last night froze hard - cleared off  about 9 o clock and thawed freely until late in the afternoon -yet the wind blew hard as was extremely perceing as we passed over widely extended pararais at some time there was nota tree or shrub within our vew these vast pararais ere dry – roaling  - fertile and better watered than usual - The children in the Waggons ware much chilled and wept bitterly – one them when taken out this evening appeared near being chilled to death  A young man died last night of a lingering consumption - having two corpses to bury this morning the Indians refused to move forward until after the burial – But by some threats and fair promises they at length agreed to start leaving a few to bury the dead - It was now between 11 & 12 o clock and we ware obliged to travel 12 miles or get neither forage or provisions it was near sundown when we pitched our tents in lewises grove hungary and cold – the Major part of the detachment did not arrive until*

*It rained and snowed so much that the Indians would not travel.*

49

*after dark – It is truely pittyable to here*
*the children crying with hunger and cold*
*and to see the woman shivering gropeing*
*their way in the dark through brush to*
*find a spot to build a fire and stretch a*
*tent over the snow - A little upwards of*
*20 bushels corn for 300 horses - beaf was*
*isued after dark but no flower – loud*
*complaints are heard-many do not arrive*

## November 23, 1832

*Cold and clear and cold this morning but*
*a fair prospect of a fair day - it was found*
*on examination that near half of our*
*detachment had remained in our rear*
*performing their Superrticious cerimonies*
*and burying the dead We however moved*
*early and traveled through beautiful as well*
*as Very extensive pararais in many parts*
*finely watered by springs of good water*
*some Salt as well as fresh for the last 30*
*miles the pararais are as wide as our sight*
*can extend with scattered groves of timber*
*near the watercourses  Those Parais are rich*
*beyond concepton and Coal banks are found*
*to abound in this open contry  We encamp*
*this evening at a point on the Misouria river*
*called the Petutsaw pass haveing traviled*
*from our last encampment a distance of 12*
*miles - Here is perhaps one among the most*
*beauty prospects in the western contry –*
*From this point it is believed the eye can*
*cover at one vue the largest extent of firtile*
*contry any where is to be Seen in north*
*America Near this charming spot the*
*majestic Misourie roals its turbid waters in*
*broad meanderings toward the ocean*
*offering Its bosom to the commerce of the*
*industrious and interprising*

*Traveled 15 miles.*

50

## November 24, 1832

clear and cold as yesterday this detach
moved this morning at the usual hour
and traveled to a point called tarbs
grove in Lafiette County a distance of
12 miles  The contry continues rich beyond
the conscption of those who have not seen it
and beautiful beyond discription in many
places finely watered by springs and
christial brooks meanderring through the
grass of those planes on our left timber
could not be discovered but in a few
instances through the distance traveled to
day - From a distance of 6 miles below
Petutsaw pass to Tarbs grove making 18
miles the soil appears on the banks of the
streams from 3 to 10 feet deep – the road is
in many places washed by rains 2 feet deep
without shewing a change of Soil in short
clay is nowhere to be seen – Sumack –
Plumb and hazel intermixed with a young
growth of walnut - the grove above
mentioned is said to be 6 miles across – rich
– healthy and pleasantly situated extending
to the Misourie  The Indians have lived for
two days past on hominy or rather boild corn
and beaf - Bowel complaints prevail in
camp - flour and pork obtained this evening
– spreads cheer fullness over every
countenance - hogs revd undressed and cut
up in the hair and thus distributed

We struck our tents at 8 oc and
marched until about 5. We made the
distance of 16 miles. The horses of two
of the teamsters ran away, and their
wagons were consequently left behind.

## November 25, 1832

Clear and pleasant this morning –
began to thaw briskly soon after
sunrise The grove we encampt in last
evening contains all the verieties of timber
and shrubbery common in the Western
contry - With the exception of the pekan  -
The contry continues Rich and exquisitely
beautiful finely watered & The detachment
Started earlyer this morning than usual and
travels a distance of 12 miles – to the farm
of a Mr Smith 2 ½ miles south of

A part of the detachment traveled
10 miles and the remainder
continued stationary. The wagons
which were left behind yesterday
arrived in the evening.

*Lexington the Seat of Justice for lafiette
County The old Squaw chief \*Satouvney is 5
or 6 miles in our rear this evening as usual –
no beaf or pork this evening - there is no
part of this lovely contry on which you cast
your eye but promises fair to reward the
labours of the Industrious the prospect is of
the most cheering caractor to the
philanthropic mind when it attempts to
explore the bosom of futurity and Vews in
seeming Vision the emmense population
that will in future be Sustained by the fruits
of the delightful soil over Which We travel –*

\*Satouvney, probably Squatone,
a lesser chief

## November 26, 1832

*Warm and clear weather made an early
Start and travele 10 miles to Big Snyber
creek which is swelled by the sudden
thaw of snow somuch as to be impassable –
the snow intirely disappeared to day –
We traveled through a contry rich and
in many respects Semilar in appearance
to the fine contry heretofore described - But
Springs are better & more numerous - The
pawpaw and Sumake grows over the whole
face of the contry - the further we travel the
more beautiful are the general appearances
of the grove and diversified features of this
delightful contry - in the contry Surrounding
lexington there is every appearance of health
in the general make of the contry and in the
faces of the inhabitants - beaf nor pork
cannot be obtained this evening*

*The Indians who remained behind
yesterday waiting for the teams,
joined those in front.*

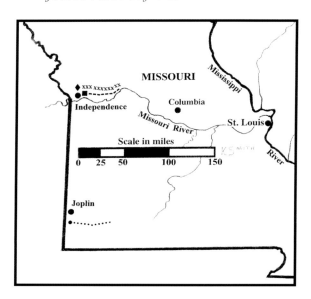

## November 27, 1832

*Warm pleasant Weather this morning the
detachment moved earlier than usual the
Swell of the water in the Snibar  produced
some delay in crossing we how ever
passed over without any accident occurring
worthy of notice and traveled 8 miles to a
branch of fire perarri creek near the farm
of Mr Shewmaker - we ware compelled to
encamp here in as much as provision and*

*We marched 10 miles.*

*forrage could not be obtained within a*
*reasonable distance if we proceeded further –*
*The contry continues equally interesting*
*and beautiful as that discribed heretofore –*
*coals are said to be plenty in this*
*neighbourhood - Several good millseats*
*are to be entered on the snibar creek*
*within from four to six miles of this point*
*We incamp within two miles of the misourie*
*river near the West boundary of Lefiette*
*County - this is charming contry certainly*
*possessing many commercial advantages*
*and well watered with Springs We are now*
*in the Vicenity of the Settlements of the*
*Morman Church - At our lodgeing I became*
*acquainted with a fine young woman whose*
*name is Moriask Mosiu – she is young –*
*intelligent - and beautiful a native of*
*the State of New york yet Strange to tell She*
*has left father Mother and friends and*
*followed mouma - improved farms can be*
*had from 4 to 5 doller per acre fire creek*
*takes Its name from the fact of 4 Indians*
*being burned up in the pararie by fireing*
*the grass*

## November 28, 1832

*A light frost this morning and a fine*
*appearance of a fair day the detachment*
*moved erly and fine Sperits haveing been*
*well fed and forraged last evening and*
*this morning We passed over a*
*contry Semilar in appearance in many*
*respects to the Contry discribed in*
*yesterdays and equally fertile travel But*
*riseing in a few Places in higher eminences*
*than any seen by us on the southside of the*
*Misourie The brows of Several of those*
*high grounds presents to View excellenct*
*quaries of lime stone and from their sides*
*isued a few good springs - At fire pararai*
*Creek is at a moderate estimate 2000 acres*
*of as fine a botom parrari a can be found in*
*any Contry covered where not burnt by the*
*late fires with grass up to our saddle scerts*

*We struck our tents at 8 oc and*
*continued traveling until late in the*
*evening, by which means we made the*
*distance of 18 miles.*

- our horses in Passing over the mellow doil
often sunk in to the dry earth up to the
posture joints - here is a Choice Situation
for a stock farm - was it not that it is
destitute of timber - the face of this pararie
exhibits a Singular apperance  - thousands
of beds of earth are thrown up by little
animals called gophers these beds are of
all Sizes from one foot square to 16 feet
square but most generally oblong and
from 5 inches to 3 feet high West of this
interesting spot are beautiful high pararais
Skerted with small improvements still
further west is a fine body of timber to
little blew river here We encampt for
the night having traveled  a distance
of 14 miles - on the East Side of Blew river
is a Very high bluff presenting a cliff
of lime Stone rocks - the land on this
stream is rich and interesting  The botom in
which we incamp contains upwards of 1000
Acres our camp is situated 1 ½ miles from
Misurie  - The inhabitants Settled in the
region of contry through which We pass are
eliterate vulgar and unpleasand in their
maners - the Scattered Settlements produced
by the scarcity of timber will necessarily
give the riseing generation a semiler cast –
the towns however furnish an exception to
this Vew - Last night at a late hour a young
man came into the lodgeing Swearing by
god that he was a right ranting ringtailed
roarer after considerable altercation with
the landlady and comeing near to get himself
saluted With the pokeing Stick he tumbled
into bed With the Child on the floor and laid
until morning - here is a correct Sample of
many in the contry

## November 29, 1832

The weather fine and warm this morning
ade.
the detachment Moved Early as usual
and crossed the fine and extensive botom
of blew river this bottom runs down to

We traveled 13 miles to the Gascon-

*Misourie is principally Pararie*
*diversified with handsome litte grove Which*
*much encreas its beauty its fertility is equal*
*to any thing of the kind heretofore seen and*
*contains Several 1000 Acres We then*
*entered a high land timbered contry rich and*
*well watered by Small Springs for 8 miles to*
*the Village of indipendance this village*
*appears altogether healthy and prosperour*
*traveled four miles further through land of*
*fine quality and encampt having traveled*
*12 miles*

## November 30, 1832

*Warm and cloudy our encampment being*
*within 14 miles of the shawney Village*
*great anxiety prevailed in the detachment*
*for an early start fires ware kindled long*
*before day and loud notices given to hurry*
*breakfast preparitory to our march and for*
*the first time on our whole tour the Indians*
*seemed to hurry their conducters - Many*
*set off before the public waggons - We*
*traveled a rich timbered contry finely*
*watered with Springs and abounding*
*more in oak timber than any heretofore*
*described - from indipendance to the*
*boundary of the state is settled prencipally*
*by the Morema Church - their lands are*
*parceled out by the bishop in small tracts*
*according to the number of family able*
*to labour - in these lands a life estate*
*only is Vested and only on condition of*
*remaining member of the church - There*
*seems to be a great lack on inteligence*
*among this people - Plain and coars in their*
*dress – their maners appear gentle and*
*inoffensive to travelers the great body of*
*this misguided people seem to be in destitute*
*circumstances - It is also said by respectable*
*authority that they hold indiscrimate sexual*
*intercourse without regard to matrimonial*
*rites - limited only by the pale of the church –*
*Blew river is a fine mill stream - a beautiful*
*contry continues to the village above stated*

*The Indians remained to-day for the*
*purpose of waiting for some of their*
*brethren who are behind.*

at which we arrived late in the evening –
Misted rain in the after part of the day - The
Indians meet their frinds with cheerful
countenances - Pass complements and camp
near the town

## December 1, 1832

last night rained and froze a scarcity of
wood made our situation in camp quite
fortable - daylight presented the
whole face of the contry covered over
with ice the timber was so loaded with
ice as to make it dangerous to pass through
the Surrounding forest - continued to rain
and thaw through the day - the inclemency
of the weather prevented us from dowing
any business to day except that of Isuing
the necessary provisions - The Shawney
village consists of 16 houses is called corn
stalk town - It stands on a high bluff near
a good little stream sufficient to turn a mill
many of the Indians live on small farms the
number before the late immigration is said
to be 400 the additon now made is 334
Shawneys - the ottaways are 80 in number –
left the camp alone

It commenced raining in the night and
continued all day, so that the uncom-
detachment could not travel.

## December 2, 1832

the morning appeared fair and warm –
the Sleet intirely disappeared and the day
remained fine Mr Merit Mr Meridith &
self repaired early to the camp and
commenced distributing tent cloaths to
those Indians who had most need of them
this took up the principal part of the day
Col Abert & Mj Pool compromised wi the
nation for losses on the way by giveing
the public horses 22 in number and horse
geers on hand as a compensation in full –
We bid farewell With this people forever
and turned our faces Gladly toward home
and thus ended an emmigration of 74 days
on the road –

We were compelled to cross a stream
several times to-day which nearly
swam the horses, so that we were my-
detained along the road so much, that
we traveled but 8 miles.

On December 3, 1832, Richard Cummins, U.S. Indian Agent, certified that 72 Ottawa Indians from Ocquinoxcy Village and Blanchard Fork, Ohio, were turned over to his agency by Col. J. J. Abert.

## December 3, 1832

[no entry for this day]

We traveled 14 miles. One keg of powder 100 lbs of lead were given to the Indians to-day, by Lt. Lane upon

the condition that they should pay for it in game which should be divided among all as other supplies of provisions.

## December 4, 1832

we left the town of Indipendance - fair weather and bounded over the beautiful Pararis down the Misourie untill we arrived at St charls here our Capt Weaver and myself gave them a hearty shake of the hand and made the best of our way to alton on Mississippi where we arrived early next day without making any delay we passed on through Edwardsville – Greenville to Vandalia at which place we arrived late in the evening of the 13th December on the 14 rain commenced falling briskly and continued through the day at this point capt weaver and myself parted and bid each other farewell with all the good feelings which had hitherto existed between us and I took the way through Shelbyville Myres is west of this place in this place the lanlord gave me a humourous account of capt Robb he (said the land lord) came trailing along after the Indians in front - leaving the party given him in charge to Shift for themselves – complained that he was extremely Ill or had been ill – called for warm water to bathe his feet - said he never drank any thing - eat a harty supper - took a dram and became cheerful - grew poorly – had the sheets of his bed aired before lying down to rest - declared Vehemently that he would stop the whole immigration until the Indians should be

We traveled 20 miles to-day. We with started early, had a good road, and traveled late.

*collected together - Was willing to be*
*understood to be the soul and core of the*
*whole immigration - I Was much amused with*
*the inkeepers account of which the above is*
*only notes*

*On December 5, 1832, Richard Cummins, U.S. Indian Agent, certified that 334 Shawnee Indians were turned over to his agency from the Hog Creek and Wahpahkonnetta Ohio by Col. J. J. Abert.*

### December 5, 1832

*We traveled 13 miles to-day, which brought us to White river.*

### December 6, 1832

*We remained at the encampment for the purpose of refreshing the detachment.*

### December 7, 1832

*About 11 oc we left the encampment and crossed the White river, and marched 9 miles beyond it – making 10 miles to-day.*

### December 8, 1832

*We traveled 12 miles, to Gibson's fork of the Neosho.*

### December 9, 1832

*We traveled 15 miles.*

### December 10, 1832

*We traveled 7 miles today. We could have gone further, but it was necessary to halt to get corn and meat.*

### December 11, 1832

*We traveled 13 miles.*

## December 12, 1832

*We traveled 18 miles today.*

## December 13, 1832

*We traveled 12 miles to the Seneca Agency.*

*I delivered the Indians into the care of Maj. Kennerly, the agent for the Seneca, agreeably to in instruction. They will remain upon the land of their brethren, the Seneca, until an exchange of their tract of land is made, at which time they will remove, to the piece given them.*

*I & my Assistant, with the chiefs and other of our detachment went to examine their tract which is situated west of the Neosho, and does not extend within less than five or six miles of it. But in consequence of its being too high to ford we were compelled to remain on the E side. There was no boat in which we could cross.*

*The resident Seneca say it cannot be cultivated – that there is scarcely any timber upon it, and but little good soil – and withal, entirely unadapted to their purpose.*

*Upon this representation they refused going to see it, but they have since been over to make an examination of its advantages and disadvantages, but what their conclusion is I have not yet learned.*

*Daniel M. Workman*
*Condt of Lew. Em. Ind.*

*By Daniel R. Donihue*

*Silversmiths Son & wife were numbered in the family of the Widow Turtle, but on route separated from them.*

*One child died while on the route belonging to the family of the Tall Mans Widow.*

*By the various changes made during the route it will be perceived that there are now but 220 persons.*

*Daniel R. Donihue*
*Enrolling Agent*

## December 15, 1832

*lay at Wabash point the pararai*
*West of this point is 16 miles long from*
*4 to 10 miles wide - rich and level –*
*traveled through it in the night - had*
*many fears*

Shelby is on his way home.

# December 16, 1832

*Warm and rainy*

# TRIPS

Seneca of the Sandusky River

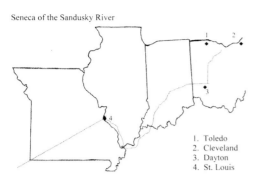

1. Toledo
2. Cleveland
3. Dayton
4. St. Louis

Hog Town/Wapakoneta
Seneca/Shawnee Lewistown
Oquanoxa's Village
Blanchard's Fork

A. Entire 1832 People
B. Seneca/Shawnee of Lewistown
C. Ottawa and Shawnee

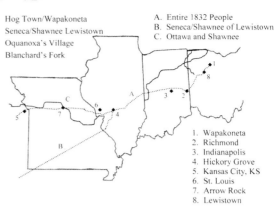

1. Wapakoneta
2. Richmond
3. Indianapolis
4. Hickory Grove
5. Kansas City, KS
6. St. Louis
7. Arrow Rock
8. Lewistown

Ottawa

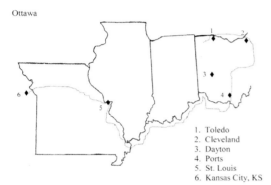

1. Toledo
2. Cleveland
3. Dayton
4. Ports
5. St. Louis
6. Kansas City, KS

Wyandotte

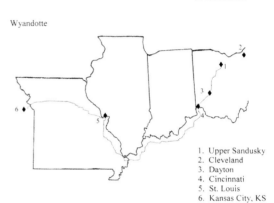

1. Upper Sandusky
2. Cleveland
3. Dayton
4. Cincinnati
5. St. Louis
6. Kansas City, KS

On January 5, 1833, Col. J. J. Abert filed the following report to Secretary of War, Lewis Cass:

*Washington, January, 5th 1833*

*Hon. Lewis Cass*
  *Secretary of War*

*Sir:*

  *I have the honor to report- that in conformity with your instructions of the Oct 3 I left this city on Oct 5 and arrived at Urbana, Ohio on the 11th of October*
  *Having ascertained that the emigration Expedition of Indians from the State of Ohio, was then on the way to the West, and has been several days on the journey, and not upon a stage road, I left Urbana on the 13th of October in pursuit of them.*
*I moved with all the speed which such a mode of traveling admits, overtaking the rear detachments about five miles west of the Wabash and the final detachment with which I found Col. Gardiner on the 25th of October, at Hickory Grove, within about forty miles of the Mississippi.*
*This detachment has halted here in order to give time to those in the rear to come up, and in order to make arrangements for that part of the emigration destined to the Neosha, and which would probably be separated from the main body at this place. Col. Gardiner had written to Gen. Clark, Superintendent of Indian Affairs at St. Louis, for information and advice on this subject.*
  *As is well known to you, the great object of my mission was to get this emigration to its destination this season, and if possible to resolve the differences, which were known to exist between the special agent and the disbursing officer, and which differences were considered as hazarding the emigration.*
  *These differences I found had originated in different views which each had given to his own instructions, and which from that origin, had extended into such decided personalities, that no personal intercourse whatever, not even in relation to their duties existed between them. It was soon evident to my judgement that reconciliation was impossible and without-reconciliation and harmonious action, the emigration would in all human probability fail for that season.*
  *In relation to the merit of these differences and of the various accusations official and personal, made by each against the other I did not enquire. I saw clearly that any investigation on this subject would involve me in a most unpleasant labyrinth, waste that time which we had not to spare, and in the end produce results satisfactory to no one. I determined therefore at once, to leave any investigation which might thought necessary to other hands and a more convenient season and to give the whole of my efforts to the direction of the emigration.*
  *Whatever may have been the differences between these agents in relation to the authority of each, with that with which I was invested there could be none. It was paramount to the authority of any other agent of the emigration and adequate to the object with which I considered myself especially charged. But it was an authority which I could not delegate, and as its exercise was necessary that I should remain with the emigration in order to exercise*

*it.*

Under all these considerations I decided to take the direction of the emigration into my own hands and accordingly on the morning of the 27th being that of the second day after I had overtaken the special agent, I assumed the direction of the emigration and thus became responsible for its successful termination.

The Special Agent, Col. Gardiner, was thus immediately invited to accompany me as far at least as the Mississippi and to aid me in the duties I had undertaken, by his information and advice, and it is no more than justice to him to acknowledge, that he accepted of this invitation with the greatest cheerfulness, rendering to me the most efficient and valuable service, in the most polite and gentleman like manner. In fact to the many valuable ideas, which I acquired from him during the few days of our association, in relation to the Indian character generally and to that of this emigration in particular, as well as to that of the several agents attached to it, may be attributed much of the success which afterward attended my efforts.

On the 28th all of the rear detachments had arrived, and on the 29th of October the party destined for the Neosho was started under the direction of General Workman, who has been the principal conductor of the Neosbo detachment to this place. I added an additional assistant conductor to this party in the person of Mr. James Workman, a highly efficient and able man, and who had accompanied me from Urbana at my request. This party was made particularly strong in its agents, as it had to separate from us, intending myself to accompany the main body destined for the vicinity of the Kansas.

As a division of the emigration had to now take place, I applied to Gen. Atkinson for an officer to serve as a additional disbursing agent, in order to preserve to the Department the usual military responsibility for expenditures with the greatest promptness, he detached for the purpose, that experienced and valuable officer Capt. T C. Palmer, who as soon as he arrived was place on duty with the large detachment, which I accompanied, and Lt. Lane was ordered to proceed as the disbursing officer, to the smaller detachment, destined for the Neosho.

While at Hickory Grove Mr. Robb the principal conductor of the Shawnee having been some time seriously indisposed, resigned his place and Judge Shelby, assistant- conductor to the same party and highly deserving of the distinction was immediately and by the advice of Col. Gardiner promoted to fill the vacancy.

On the morning of the 30 we moved with the main body toward the Mississippi, the vicinity of which we reached on the evening of the 31st, and passed over the river, on the 1st and 2nd day of November. This large detachment of the emigration being now west of the Mississippi, Col. Gardiner, the Special Agent, who has hitherto remained with me, took his departure for his home under a leave of absence.

Having myself no failing in relation to this duty but those eminating from an anxious desire that it should be successfully terminate during the present season and having experienced great advantage from advice and remarks of Col. Gardiner, I decided it no more than justice to Government as well as to him, to invite him to continue with me, if consistent with his feelings, to the termination of the expedition. He however declined the invitation. Stating his reason in a letter and returned home, as I before remarked upon a leave of absence. Major Pool the Assistant Special Agent, was then requested to take upon himself the direction of all details.

Without enumerating the many embarrassments which we experienced during the march, as well from the composition of the emigration as from the Cholera which attacked the detachment of the Ottaways, I will briefly state that we commenced crossing the Mississippi on the 1st of November, which occupied 2 days, arrived at the Missouri at Arrow Rock on the sixteenth and were there detained five days in crossing the detachment and by a violent storm of wind, rain, sleet, and snow, but in the end, were so fortunate as to reach the Shawnee Village twenty miles west of the Town of Independence, during the afternoon of the 30th of November, which after deducting the delays before stated, was completing the entire march of 320 miles in 23 days.

I cannot speak too highly of the conduct and exertion of Mr. Pool, the Assistant Special Agent, and all the conductors attached to the emigration. They were animated by the most ardent zeal, to get this emigration through as early as possible, and were gratified by seeing their efforts crowned with most happy success, before the inclemency of the winter came to oppress if not defeat us.

It gives me pleasure also to state that the party under Gen. Workman destined for the Neosho was when last heard from within about 150 miles of its home, which it had without doubt safely reached long before now.

Being fully aware that disquietudes and many of them well grounded---with the main body which were conducted to the vicinity of the Kansas. I determined before leaving them, if possible by any reasonable arrangement, to appease these disquietudes and to leave the Indians as satisfied with the treatment extended toward them as they evidently were with the appearance of their new land. For this purpose I had first all the Shawnee Chiefs called together, and in the presence of the agents resident with them as well as those who had been employed in conducting them to their new homes. I expressed to them the great pleasure I felt at the fortunate and early termination of the emigration. Then alluding to the losses which they had sustained during the route and the desire I felt from the known paternal feelings of their great father in the President towards them, to fulfill in the most liberal spirit the Treaty in relation to their emigration. I offered in lieu of and in full compensation of all their losses, to give to them the public horses yet remaining, and which had been used in the emigration of their tribe, and also the several sets of wagons gears and public saddles which had been similarly used. These to be received by them in lieu of their losses during the march and such as any part of the articles stipulated in the treaty.
I also stated to them that the feeding under the treaty would commence on the 1st of January 1833, but in the mean time they would be fed as usual at the expense of the United States.

To prevent any misunderstanding on these subjects I had the proposal twice explained and interpreted by that able interpreter Mr. Shane, and as many of the chiefs spoke English well, there can be no doubt that the whole matter was correctly understood.
The chiefs after a consultation with each other, accepted them freely upon the conditions stated. A statement of the agreement was afterward reduced to writing, having no means of writing at hand at that time, and herewith accompanies this report

The chiefs then desired me to state to you their great anxiety to have the special tract of 100,000 acres, intended for their use surveyed as early as possible, and also that that the farming utensils and the various tools provided for in the treaty might be delivered as early as possible. They wished to accompany the commissioner in the survey, and were particularly anxious that the mill sites should be selected, as their desire is to establish their permanent residences, as conveniently accessible to these as possible.

*The Chief Perry of the Shawnee Village, and of the tribe removed thirteen some years since, desired me to assure you that he had rigidly followed the advice of his great father in cultivating peace and harmony with all the adjacent tribes, between whom and the Shawnee, there existed the most cordial and friendly intercourse- That his people are generally separated upon distinct tracts, cultivating the soil, and were contented and comfortable. On the next day I held a council for similar purpose with the small band of Ottawa which formed a part of the emigration. This band is connected by intermarriage with the Shawnees of Waughpachennatta, look up to them as an "Elder brother" and accompanied them in the emigration.*

*Their particular section of land was selected about forty miles from the Shawnee Village, and stranger to them. The Shawnees have invited them to remain in the vicinity of the village until this Spring, which they were extremely desirous of doing, contemplating the course of sending an exploring party upon their land during the winter, to select the spot upon which they were ultimately to settle. This was stated to me by the chiefs in council, with an expression of their strong desire to be indulged. So reasonable a desire was not opposed by me, and particularly as I was assured by the agent, Major Cummins, that they could be fed with much more certainty near the village, and could be much more carefully watched over, no special agent being yet appointed to attend to them and they on that account being placed under his care.*

*I then also proposed to the chiefs, the same remuneration for their losses which had been proposed to the Shawnee, adding however, that in consideration of permitting them to remain near the Shawnee Village, they were remove themselves to their new lands about forty miles distant, at their own expense, as soon as the weather would admit.*

*The chiefs then complained of the disappointment in not yet receiving the 200 dollars stipulated to be paid in the Treaty, urged me to make some arrangement by which they should be paid at least a part of this sum, as it was absolutely necessary to meet their present wants. Fully aware of this and of the poverty of this tribe, I obtained three hundred dollars from the agent and paid it to them as a part of the 200 dollars stipulated in the treaty. The whole arrangement was then reduced to writing and signed by the chiefs and by myself and I am happy to add that it gave to them great satisfaction.*

*Having now completed all the assignments to which appeared to me necessary, in order to heal the disquituded which had existed with these Indians. Having seen them contented and preparing their lodges for Winter, and the contractors on the ground and furnishing them with provisions. I consider myself as having fulfilled the duty which had been committed to me and I took my departure from them, leaving them under the care of Major Cummins the resident agent and Major Campbell his assistant, gentlemen whose intelligence, knowledge of their duties and efficiency and benevolence of character could leave no doubt that the government would be faithfully served and the Indians kindly and correctly attended to.*

*On my return I stopped at St. Louis and duly informed Gen. Clark the Supt of Indian Affairs, of all the arrangements herein spoken of, furnishing him with duplicates of such as has been reduced to writing and then set out for this place, where I arrived the 30th of December, and on the 1st of January 1833, again resumed the duties of my office.*

*With this report I have the honor to enclose*

*1. The agreement alluded to between the Shawnee and myself on behalf of the United States*

*2. Similar agreement with the Ottawa*

*3. A receipt from the Ottawa for 300 dollars*

*4. A receipt from the Shawnee for 25 new rifles delivered to them at Arrow Rock on the Missouri. These are the rifles provided for in the Treaty with the Shawnee and which were received at Arrow Rock and delivered there.*

> *Respectfully Submitted*
> *By sir,*
> *Your obedient Servant*
> *J. J. Abert Lt. Col U.S.A.*
> *and Special Commissioner of the*
> *Emigration*

On February 25, 1833, James B. Gardiner filed the following report to the Secretary of War, Lewis Cass.

*To the Hon. Lewis Cass*
> *Secretary of War*

*Sir*

*In compliance with your letter of the 6th inst. requiring me to submit to you a detailed report of my proceedings, from the commencement of my appointment, and also a return showing the number of Indians left in Ohio, their position, the reason why they did not remove with the party taken by me, and my views respecting the propriety of removing them at the public expense — I have the honor to present the following material.*

*Previously to my departure from this city, in April last, I received your verbal orders, under the sanction of the President, to proceed to the several Indian Reservations, in the state of Ohio, as soon as practicable after my return home, for the purpose of notifying the respective tribes, that the treaties formed with them had been ratified by the Government, and suitable arrangements would soon be made for their removal and the supply of the various articles promised them.*

*Accordingly, I set out on the * of May for the Indian towns, and soon afterward, held preparatory councils with the Chiefs of the Seneca, Shawnees, and Ottawas. They appeared pleased with the prospects before them and promised to use all deligence putting together several tribes, the Indians expressed a strong desire to be permitted to travel by land and take their horses with them. They were assured that the Government would not object to this course, but would gratify all their reasonable wishes.*

*At the preparatory council, referred to, the subject was again mentioned and I was reminded by the chiefs, of the promises made to them during the rendering of their treaties. Knowing that you thought it inexpedient to remove them by land I could now only promise them that I would communicate their request to yourself and the President, and hoped they would still be permitted to remove in the way they most desired.*

*Before leaving the Indian country, I received your letter of the 17th of May, which required me as soon as I had completed a tour among the several bands," to submit to the Department a "project for the operation of the season," in which I was instructed to state the number and duties of the persons necessary to be employed as assistants in the emigra-*

tion, and suggest the names of such as I might think proper to employ. I was further direct-ed to state the route, which I thought should be taken, the number of parties which should move separately, the time they ought assemble, the mode of supplying, and any other ideas which might occurred to me, by which the Government would be enabled to direct in the best manner the general operation.

In accordance with these instructions, I prepared, as much in detail as possible, a "proj-ect operations for the season", embracing the several points referred to in my consider-ations. This document was dated and transmitted on the 23rd of June. I therein stated that, "in the exercise of the discussion confided to me in the printed instructions of the Depart-ment, of the 13th ultimo. I have chosen the route by land as the most congenial to the habits and comfort of the Indians and probably not much, if any, more expensive to the Govern-ment." I considered it more certain and less liable to sickness and accidents.

Before submitting my project, however, I addressed your letter on the 2nd of June, stating the wish of the Indians to travel by land, in referring to which, in your answer of the 21' of June, you say, "The President, with whom I have conferred on the subject cannot accede to the proposition. Gen. Gibson will advise you of the result."

On the 28th of June, Gen. Gibson wrote me as follows: "On the subject of the removal by land, as again adverted to in your letter to me, I will remark that the determination of the President remains unaltered. If they [the Indians} in reality entertain the fears to which you allude, you will endeavor to correct their impressions." Tell them of the rapidity and certainty with which they will travel, of the distress to which the Seneca who removed last year were subjected, and use any other arguments which occur to your mind: but above all say that the plan of removal by  steam boats is unalterable."

In compliance with these orders, I went again among the Indians, and used every persua-sion in my power, to induce them to accede to the decision of the President. My efforts were utterly unavailing. And I so informed the Commissary General of Subsistence in a detailed report of the 23rd of July.

As the season advanced I made a third attempt to change the determination of the Chiefs and their people. But the Cholera, had by this time made its appearance in steam boats on the Lakes and on the northern borders of Ohio, and the Indians became firmly resolved to remain on their lands another year rather than run the risk of contracting the prevailing epidemic in traveling by water.

My own efforts were ably seconded by my several assistants, in their visits of business among the tribes, but their exertions were equally unsuccessful.

Believing from my knowledge of the Indian character, and of the sinister influence exer-cised by some of the traders among the Ohio tribes, that it would be impossible to induce them to remove by water to St. Louis in sufficient time to accomplish the remainder of their journey (which must necessarily be by land) before the cold weather would prevent them, from traveling: I felt anxious that the President should change his first decision, and permit the adoption of the land route.

Accordingly, I addressed the Commissary General of Subsistence on the subject, on the 23rd of July, and requested that my letter might be laid before the President. I received an answer from the Acting Commissary General, date the 31 of July, and was informed that the President, the Secretary of War, and Commissary General were all absent from the city of Washington: but that the Acting Secretary of War would transmit my letter to the President, in Tennessee.

About the 10th of September, while in the vicinity of the Seneca Indians, I received a letter from the Acting Commissary General of the l of September covering a  letter from the President, dated at the Hermitage on the 17thof August, in which Permission was given to remove the Indians by land.

During the whole this time, that is from the middle of May, until the 10th of September,  I was unable to make any efficient preparation, or to adopt any definite course in the removal. I did indeed, at my own personal risk, order the purchase of seventy-five horses for the service, a few days before the receipt of the President's letter, but adopted this measure as the only possible means of removing the Indians during the year 1832, even with the consent of the President to take the route by land. The advanced period of the season rendered it extremely doubtful whether with every practicable exertion and facility, we should be able to accomplish so long a journey, with such a mixed multitude of Indians of the worst habits, and so large a proportion of women and children among them.

The instructions to provide for the vaccination of the Indians were not received until the 10th of August. The matter, procured in Ohio, proved useless, and the attempt entirely failed. But the failure was not ascertained, until it was too late to obtain new matter from Baltimore or this city.

The blankets, sheeting and rifles, promised in the treaties, were not received until the 29th of August.

The payment of the sum of $19,000 to the Shawnees and Senecas, for their improvements, was not completed until the 14th of September, owing to the non-arrival of the money for that purpose.

The payment of the customary annuities to the Ottawas was not made until after their arrival at the rendezous, ten miles north of Piqua, on the 25th of September. This was owing to an inadvertence on the part of Gov. Porter of Michigan.

I have thus briefly stated the principal causes, which delayed the final departure of the expedition to so late a period as the 26th of September. But there were numerous other and apparently unavoidable causes, which contributed to the delay, and were of a most vexatious and embarrassing nature. And to these may be added the proverbial indolence of Indians on such occasions, and the habitual and excessive intemperance's of the half civilized bands who have lived so long contiguous to the white settlements of Ohio.

For the sake of convenience, as well as to avoid collisions and quarrels on the way, each tribe, or band, was marched separately, and, as nearly as circumstances would permit, from ten to twenty miles apart. While passing through the populous settlements, it was found impossible to prevent the Indians from obtaining ardent spirits in such quantities as produced some serious disturbances and numerous detentions.

About the 1st of October the several detachments crossed the western line of the State of Ohio into Indiana. The precise number of the emigrants I could never ascertain, while on the march, in consequence of the constant inter course between the tribes, their habits of visiting each other alternately, for days together, their practice of scattering along the road, or through the woods, or remaining in the villages, where whisky could be procured. Some seventy or eighty of the Shawnee s remained at Wapaphkonnetta, after the main body had left the rendezous near Piqua, and Capt. Robb was ordered to return and bring them on. They did not overtake the Detachment, until we arrived within forty miles of the Mississippi. Nor could I until now, tell the number of the Shawnees who remained on the Hog Creek Reservation, and refused to remove with their band. But I suppose the whole number

68

removed last year from Ohio to have been about eight hundred. The most of them traveled on horseback. A few had carriages and wagons of their own. The sick, the aged, and decrepit, who were unable to ride on horses, were carried in the public baggage wagons, in a comfortable manner.

Until we arrived at Indianapolis, in Indiana, the Indians were supplied with rations by contract, according to the printed regulations of the Department. But this mode, besides being by at least one third the most expensive, and subjecting us to frequent frauds, could not be kept up, while on the march, without much inconveniences, delay and uncertainty. It was therefore deemed expedient to order the necessary provisions to be supplied in bulk, on the requisition of the respective Conductors, when neither the Assistant Agent nor myself were present. Flour and meal were procured in bags, or barrels, and beef or pork on foot. This was much more satisfactory to the Indians, who selected their own distributors, and divided according to the necessities, and not the number in each family. They butchered the cattle, receiving the hide and tallow for their labour, with which they purchased coffee, sugar, spices and other necessary articles for the sick and aged of their women. I soon became convinced of the sufficiency of the Indian nation, as fixed by the Department, and while rations were issued according to numbers, many families had large surplus of flour and beef, particularly the former, which they would sometimes sell to persons along the road when prevented from putting it in the public wagons.

In the three detachments, there were about five hundred horses belonging to the Indians and seventy-five purchased by the United States. The latter were very improperly selected, many of them incurably diseased and most of them either too poor or too old for such service. They were not such as were ordered and were purchased at a higher price than was stipulated by me. The consequence was, that the public horses, though fed with grain and hay, were unable to sustain the fatigues of the journey, and many of them died, or failed on the road; while the Indian horses with few exceptions, were kept in good traveling order on tame and wild pasturage.

At Indianapolis about the 5th or 6th of October, the Disbursing Agent gave me written notice that he was "out of funds, and the emigration must stop" until money could be procured, He returned to Cincinnati for funds. I continued the march of the Indians without an hours delay on this account. On the 24th of October the front Detachment arrived at Hickory Grove, in Boyd County, Illinois, and within forty miles of St. Louis, a distance of more than two hundred miles, the whole of which was traveled in twenty days, with about eight hundred Indians and six hundred horses supported principally on money borrowed from the Indians themselves. Here we remained for three or four days to recruit the horses, and await the return of an express I had sent to Gen. Clark at St. Louis, to obtain information relative to the best route by which we could avoid the region infected with the Cholera, which was then prevailing with great malignity at St. Louis.

While thus detained, Col. John J. Abert, of the Topographical Engineers, came up with us, charged with instructions from you, relative to the future progress of the expedition. The Disbursing Agent arrived the next day, with a partial supply of money.

It is unnecessary, if not improper for me in this place, to advert to the circumstances, which, in the opinion of the Acting Secretary of War, rendered the interposition of Col. Abert necessary to the restoration of that harmony and concert of action, essential to the success of the service. It is but just, however, to say that I found him a gentleman of the highest sense of honor, cool, firm, impartial and intelligent, and in every respect adequate to the delicate and important duties assigned him. In what manner He executed the instructions of the Department his own report; I have no doubt will furnish the best and most ample testimony.

After I had received permission to return to my family in Ohio, Col. Abert expressed a wish that I would accompany him to the Mississippi, before relinquishing the charge of the expedition. I readily complied, and felt it a pleasure, as well as a duty, to afford him every, assistance in my power, in becoming acquainted with the numerous and complicated details of the service, which could only be learned by experience and practice. His own good sense, however, conciliatory disposition, and energy of character, furnished the surest guarantee of his entire efficiency in performing the arduous duties he was about to undertake. And the result, I am happy to know, has fully realized my warmest anticipation. Having accompanied Col. Abert to the eastern bank of the Mississippi at Alton, and witnessed the crossing of the main body of the Indians, I left the expedition on the 2 of November, and returned to my residence, from whence I have had the honor to report to you for further orders.

I have considered it unnecessary to go further into the details of my proceedings, than I have done, either or to the preparatory or progressive measures, as they are already in the possession of the Department, in the several communications which I have from time to time, had the honor to address to yourself and the Commissary General of Subsistence, and to these I beg leave to refer to you, particularly the following, and to ask that they may be appended to this report, whenever it shall become necessary to lay it before Congress or the President:

1st   My letters to you at the 22nd and27th of August, and 1st, 8th and 21st of Octo ber 1832.
2nd   My letters to the Commissary General of Subsistence, of the 23rd of July the 29th of August and the3rd and 8th of October 1832.
3rd My letter to Gen. Wm. Clark, of the 25th of October (herewith transmitted)

It gives me much satisfaction to say that from the Assistant Agent, the Conductors, and Assistant Conductors, with a single exception, I received every support and assistance I could have wished or expected. They were faithful, efficient, and indefatigable in the discharge of their respective duties. Capt. David Robb, the Conductor of the Shawnee Detachment was unable to perform any active or laborious duty, by reason of infirmity and indisposition. It would have been better for the service, if he had seen the propriety of resigning, when first appointed.

In answer to your enquiries as to the number of the Indians left in Ohio-their position, the reason why they did not remove with the party taken by me, and my views respecting the propriety of removing them at the public expense: I have the honor to inform you that the number remaining, a great proportion of who are women and children, is eighty-four. They belong to what is called the Hog Town band of Shawnees, and are generally sober, discreet and industrious persons. They determined to remain until next Spring, rather than travel in company with the Shawnees of Wapaghkonnetta, Who they believe have treated them unjustly on several occasions, and might again defraud and quarrel with them on the way. When they made known to me their intention of remaining, I gave them no assurance that they would receive any assistance from the Government, if they did not remove at the same time with the rest of their brethren. But from their uniform good character, and the moral example they have always exhibited to their tribe, I think it would be just and proper that

they should be assisted at the public expense, in their removal. And as they are defenseless against injury and imposition, and must pass through that part of the State of Illinois,
where from the unforgotten occurrences of the last year, a strong feeling of hostility exists
against all Indians, I respectfully recommend that they may be placed under the charge
and protection of some Competent and experienced Conductor, acquainted with the route,
and capable of making purchases for them and defending them against fraud and violence.
They have horses and wagons of their own, and will, of necessity, as well as choice, remove
by land.
  I have the honor to be,
 With great respect
  Your mo.Obd. Sevt.
   James B. Gardiner
    Spel. Agt. & Supdt.

Washington City
  February25th 1833

# Chapter 4 – Final Thoughts

The story of "A Sorrowful Journey" recorded in the official documents and Shelby's journal tells only a small portion of the story. Only a hint of the turmoil, the problems and the hardships of the individuals, is gleaned from time to time. Only when the written bits and pieces of the record are looked at in a frame of reference of the writers and the victims can it be hoped to understand the reality of "A Sorrowful Journey."

People responsible for the action that took place and writing it for the official version produce the records of the government. Whether they were sympathetic to the situation or merely recording the events to satisfy their duty is hard to judge. The diary and journal that were not to be sent as official records hint at a different slant on the journey. The feelings expressed by non-participants shortly after the journey have even a more sympathetic view to the plight of the Indians. The absence entirely of the feelings and records by the Indians themselves creates the crux of the issue, the depth and extent to the title "A Sorrowful Journey," sorrowful that it had to take place, sorrowful for the people, sorrowful for the way it was handled, and sorrowful for the way it was recorded.

The major sources of the written records are James B. Gardiner, Special Superintendent and Commissioner of the Emigration; J. J. Abert, Special Commissioner of the Emigration; Daniel Workman, Conductor of the Seneca/Shawnee Detachment; Daniel R. Dunihue, Assistant Conductor of the Seneca/Shawnee Detachment. Other sources are the letters between the Secretaries of the War that were served during this period: Lewis Cass; Acting Secretary John Robb; the Commissary General for Subsistence George Gibson; Acting Commissary General J. H. Hook; Lt. J. Lane, the Disbursing Agent for the Emigration; and other correspondence in the Record Group 75 in the National Archives cited in the bibliography.

The written sources not produced for the government are the correspondence of Daniel R. Dunihue, Assistant Conductor of the Seneca/Shawnee Detachment, and the journal of Judge John Shelby, who was the Assistant Conductor of the Shawnee Detachment and later the Conductor of the Shawnee and Ottawa Detachments.

Accounts written by non-participants are History of the Shawnee Indians by Henry Harvey and newspaper accounts cited in the bibliography.

The key people, the Native Americans, in the journey and their side of the story will never be reviewed or analyzed by contemporary investigators. The Euro-American key people and their records are our only source. Except for a few, very little is known about them and their role and attitudes at the time of our story.

The detached people, Andrew Jackson, Lewis Cass, George Gibson and minor governmental officials, were all hundreds of miles away from the journey and depended upon communications from the on-site factions. Their major obligation was to get the job done and in almost all cases it was the first time for this to be done. Jackson, the President, wanted the removal accomplished at the lowest cost and in the easiest manner, which was by water in his opinion. He had very little compassion for the Native Americans and their plight. Lewis Cass, Secretary of War, had a long history of dealing with the Indians in Ohio. His previous associations and actions demonstrated a reasonably fair awareness of their plight. George Gibson, the Commissary General for Subsistence, had a one track mindset: Do it in the least costly manner. These men reacted and were involved only in response to what was communicated to them.

The on-site people in almost all cases had several common experiences that influenced their actions. Almost all of them were frontier people who directly or through family had some associations with the Native Americans. All except Lt. J. F. Lane had been on the Ohio scene for at least a decade. Many were directly associated with the Indians in trade, reservation duties, or treaty negotiations. The key person to the emigration was James B. Gardiner, the Special Superintendent and Commissioner of the Emigration.

James B. Gardiner was a newspaperman who had entered into the political arena of Ohio. He was twice elected by the people of Green County, Ohio to the lower house of the legislature and was denied his seat by the legislature for fraudulent campaign practices. Gardiner then ran for the Senate of Ohio and served two terms. His assumed loyalty to the Jacksonian Democrats earned him a national political appointment. His name was submitted twice to Congress but each time he failed to get approval of the appointment, partially because of his alcohol problem. On his last trip to Washington, he became involved in the negotiations with the Seneca of Sandusky and their desire to remove themselves from Ohio. This experience set the stage for his appointment as Special Commissioner to the Indians of Ohio for Removal. Once the treaties were consummated, he sought and gained the appointment as Special Commissioner and Agent for the Emigration. His problem with alcohol was mentioned several times in the diaries and journals.

Colonel J. J. Abert, who became the Special Commissioner of the Emigration, was a career military person who at the time of his appointment was with the topographical unit of the army engineers. His task was to resolve the issues that were emerging on the journey and expedite the finish of the emigration. He returned to the Army Engineers after his completion of the emigration.

Lt. J. F. Lane was appointed by Gibson to make sure the expenditures were properly handled under the control of his component of the War Department. Lane was a recent graduate of West Point and appears to have had no frontier experience. The relationship between Gardiner and Lane broke down very early in the preparations for the journey. The issue centered around control of money and who had final authority.

Guy W. Pool, Assistant Superintendent, is only mentioned in other correspondence. He was Gardiner's brother-in-law and, like Gardiner, the uncle of Daniel Dunihue. Gardiner's plans for staffing were: a Conductor for each detachment, an Assistant Conductor for each detachment, an Interpreter for each, a Wagon Master for each, a group of laborers and drivers (teamsters) for each based on detachment size, and a Disbursing Agent or Commissary for each. The records reveal the following people held the various positions:

### Conductors:
Seneca/Shawnee of Lewistown

Daniel R. Workman, the son-in-law of James McPherson. McPherson was to be the Conductor until his wife's death just prior to departure. McPherson had been the Indian Agent at the Lewistown Reservation. He, as well as D. R. Workman, had witnessed the Treaty for Removal.

Shawnee of Wapakoneta and Hog Creek

David Robb, who had been the Sub-Agent at these reservations. He had witnessed the Treaty of Removal with this group and the Treaty with the Seneca/Shawnee at Lewistown. He was relieved of his duty at Hickory Grove.

Ottawa

Benjamin F. Hollister was a land speculator and Indian Trader in the Maumee Valley. He later plotted the town of Charloe, Ohio in the Reservation at Oquanoxa's Village.

## Assistant Conductors:

Seneca/Shawnee of Lewistown

Daniel R. Dunihue, the nephew of Gardiner and Pool. He would act as Gardiner's Secretary from October 16 to October 28. James Workman, the younger brother of Daniel Workman, was added to this detachment at Hickory Grove by Col. J. J. Abert.

Shawnee of Wapakoneta and Hog Creek

John Shelby, a native of Kentucky, moved to Logan County, Ohio. He had witnessed the Treaty of Removal with this group and tried to negotiate the water route for the emigration with these people. At Hickory Grove, he was elevated to Conductor of both the Shawnee and Ottawa detachments.

Ottawa

It was determined that the Ottawa did not need an Assistant Conductor because of its size.

## Interpreters:

Seneca/Shawnee of Lewistown

Martin Lane for the Seneca, who was the Interpreter at the Treaty of Removal with these people. H. H. McPherson for the Shawnee, who was the son of their Agent.

Ottawa

John King

Shawnee at Wapakoneta and Hog Creek

Joseph Park, a mixed blood member of the Hog Creek Reserve. He was to take the remaining Shawnee west in 1833. Upon the death of their Chief, John Perry, in 1845, he would become Head Chief of these people. John Reed was an Assistant Interpreter for this detachment.

## Wagon Masters:

Seneca/Shawnee of Lewistown

?

Ottawa

?

Shawnee at Wapakoneta and Hog Creek

Francis Johnson, who had witnessed their Treaty of Removal.

Mr. Calden

## Laborers:

Seneca/Shawnee of Lewistown

?

Ottawa
?
Shawnee at Wapakoneta and Hog Creek
Mr. Merritt
Mr. Meredith

**Disbursing Agent or Commissary:**
Seneca/Shawnee of Lewistown
Alexander Thomson, who had witnessed their Treaty of Removal and the Treaty of Removal with the Shawnee at Wapakoneta and Hog Creek.
Mr. Bassett
Ottawa
Samuel Vance
Shawnee at Wapakoneta and Hog Creek
W. M. Miles

Henry Harvey took charge of a Quaker school among the Shawnee in 1830 until their removal in 1832. He was one of the witnesses of the Shawnee at Wapakoneta and Hog Creek Treaty of Removal. Harvey then aided the Shawnee in their efforts to modify the treaty and gain fair compensation. He helped the Shawnee in the hearings held by Congress in regard to Gardiner's behavior in the treaty negotiations. Later he visited the Shawnee on their new reserve in 1833 and 1834 and took charge of the Quaker Mission among them in 1840. Harvey later wrote the History of the Shawnee Indians from the year 1681 to 1854, published in Cincinnati, Ohio in 1855.

The reports to the Secretary of War by Gardiner and Abert are transcribed from the originals in the National Archives as well as the excerpts from the other officials.

The emigration of the Sandusky River Seneca in 1831 was the first removal as a result of the Removal Act of 1830. The story of this emigration is full of confusion and mistakes as the War Department ventured into a series of new experiences. The constant conflict between emigration leaders in Ohio and counter actions by officials in Washington caused delay after delay and did not resolve the major problems. If it were to be any help in the preparation of the next emigration, it would be an example of what not to let happen and what course not to take. Instead, a review of the official records and the journals indicate the second emigration was in many ways a duplicate of the first in its procedure and operation.

The situation among the Indians was in a state of confusion. Opinion toward removal was far from unanimous; strong feelings existed among those who had been influenced by the Quakers' efforts. The use and abuse of alcohol, leaving the remains of family and loved ones, and the incluence of white traders all had an impact. There were no longer the strong tribal feelings that had motivated the resistance to the white persons. Among the Shawnee the old tribal divisions were the basis for division and clan chiefs (called lesser chiefs in this work). Mixed in with diversified levels of chiefs were the "old war chiefs" and orators (spokespeople) representing various factions and interests of the people. The strongest expression of unity would be demonstrated in the ceremonies before departure such as the Feast of the Dead, the Green Corn Feast, and the passing of the spirit events from the dead to the living. These prevailing conditions among the people would create a situation that made control of the emigration an overwhelming task unless rigidly supervised.

It is interesting to note the wording of the first treaty Gardiner negotiated in Ohio:

*Article VII. The said Seneca and Shawnee shall be removed to their new residence under the care and protection of some competent and proper person, friendly to them and acquainted with their habits, manners and customs; and the chiefs of the said tribes shall have the privilege of nominating such person to the President, who, if approved of by him, shall have charge of their conveyance.*

This Article does not appear in the other two ARTICLES OF AGREEMENT AND CONVENTION. Nor is there any evidence of the chiefs submitting names to the President or influencing his choice of leaders.

Gardiner in his choice of Conductors did select men who were acquainted with their habits, manners and customs. McPherson had been the Government Agent prior to removal, and when his wife died, Daniel R. Workman, his son-in-law who had lived in the area, was appointed. David Robb was a Sub-Agent with the Shawnee of Wapakoneta and Hog Creek. Benjamin Hollister had been a trader with the Ottawa for over a decade.

The existing potential problems were compounded by the delay of the emigration starting time, the distance between the action component and the decision making center, and the mode of travel and communication in 1832. Reading Shelby's journal, it becomes apparent that the supply of food for the people and their livestock was an issue before departure and would prevail throughout the emigration.

Two of the key personnel of the project were at loggerheads, James Gardiner, the Superintendent, and F. J. Lane, the Disbursing Agent. Each read into their instructions from the government powers that indicated each had final control of the disbursement of funds. Gardiner felt his orders from the Indian Office of the War Department gave him final authority. Lane felt the orders from the Commissary General of Subsistence gave him absolute control of funds and method of disbursement of food and supplies. Each sought the support of his superior in the War Department. It appears that since Gardiner had gone over the head of Gibson, the Commissary General, in regard to the appointment of Guy Pool, his brother-in-law, as the Assistant Superintendent of the Emigration; Gibson had a bias toward Lane, his appointee. The conflict between Lane and Gardiner emerged even before the start of the journey. The method of supplying the Indians and their horses instituted by Lane did not please Gardiner. Gardiner wanted this to be handled by the Disbursing Agent for each detachment. Both Lane and Gardiner were writing to their superiors about the faults of one another. As the journey progressed, so did the conflict. As early as September 29th, Dunihue in letters to his brother wrote, "Col. J.B.G. & Lieut. Lane, I understood yesterday, had a few days ago, a severe quarrel in which one struck the other – which struck I know not – no injury was sustained. One or the other (and I suppose Lane) will probably be withdrawn from the service soon. As the disharmony progresses the powers in Washington, DC, determined it was holding up the progress of the emigration. Col. J. J. Abert was dispatched to resolve the conflict with no restrictions."

There is no doubt that the weather had an ill effect on the conditions of travel and the misery of the people. Both Shelby and Workman mention frequently the rain's effect on travel and later in the journey snow, ice and cold. After severe rains, clothing and tents had to have time to dry out, delaying travel time.

The lack of funds for food and supply, either because of the conflict between Lane and Gardiner or the bureaucracy in Washington that Gardiner reported in communications, had little effect on the progress of travel. It must have created concern among the Indian leaders about the integrity of the government's role. This could have been a contributing force behind the lack of control over the emigration that Gardiner had. The lack of control is constantly mentioned in Shelby's journal and in Dunihue's diary, but in the official journal of Workman written by Dunihue, no mention is made. This lack of control was probable cause of the emigration at times having a space of eighty miles. The mixing of people of one detachment with others also indicates the weakness of regulation. There is no doubt that deaths enroute were a contributing factor. Shelby's attitude toward the Indians was mellowed because of this. His entries indicate a growing compassion for the plight of the children and women. The exposure of the people to white people on the journey was a major issue to the leadership. The casual observer, the curiosity seeker, the taunter, and the whiskey peddler all contributed to the sorrowful plight of the Indians. More than once, descriptions of these intrusions are recorded in the written records.

The extent that Gardiner's use of alcohol influenced his ability to give leadership to the overall emigration is hard to determine. His nephew, Dunihue, hints several times of the issue in the non-official records. The fact that it appears Gardiner was relieved about his dismissal of leadership by Abert and his willingness to travel to the Mississippi gives credence to the opinion that the pressure was weighing heavily upon him. In the opinion of Col. J. J. Abert, the conflict between Gardiner and Lane could not be resolved. Abert took command, relieved both men, changed leadership of two detachments, the Ottawa and Shawnee of Hog Creek and Wapakoneta, and reduced the detachments to two based on their destination. He increased the number of leaders in the Seneca/Shawnee and took command of the larger group with Pool, Shelby, Hollister and the new Disbursing Agent, Captain C. Z. Palmer.

A review of the official records and the private sources of Dunihue and Shelby indicates the role of weather, the road conditions, the spread of the emigration, the spoilage of food, the problems with the whites along the way, and lack of funds all contributed to the length and disorder of the emigration. The issue of having Gardiner as leader, the lack of control, the hardships of the Indians, the deaths and illness, and a concern for the plight of the group appear only in the private records of Shelby and Dunihue.

To the best of our knowledge, about 730 Indians started out from Wapakoneta in September, 1832. According to the official records, 636 Indians arrived at the agencies west of the Mississippi.

The Ottawa and Shawnee adjusted to their new home in Indian territory. The Quakers shortly reestablished their school and mission station among the Shawnee. Soon they were visited by two other denominations concerning establishing mission activities among them in their new homes. They built their log homes with shingled roofs and cultivated their fields. A disastrous flood hit them in 1844 and much rebuilding had to be done again. In 1853, they received the final adjustment payment for their Ohio lands.

The Kansas-Nebraska Act of 1854 forced their relocation to what is now northern Oklahoma. Once again, the people were obliged to take the final steps of their "Sorrowful Journey."

The Shawnee who refused to join the 1832 removal arranged for their emigration in the early part of 1833. In early June of 1833, they made their journey west. Even then some refused to emigrate. The balance of 67 arrived at their destination September 15, 1833, under the leadership of Joseph Parks.

Parks was a mixed blood who acted as an interpreter in all the treaty negotiations. He traveled with the 1832 group and returned to lead the 1833 group. When J.Clay, Nolesimo died, he became chief of the Wapakoneta group.

The Shawnee of Lewistown are the ancestors of Eastern Shawnee Tribe today.    The Wapakoneta/Hog Creek are the ancestors of the Shawnee Tribe today.

Twice these people were faced with a forced relocation for the benefit of a different culture. Have we not learned the "sorrowful journey" of transplanting people against their will?

# Tribal Headquarters and major concentration of population today

**Ottawa Tribe**
P.O. Box 110
Miami, OK. 74355

**Seneca-Cayuga Tribes**
P. O. Box 1283
Miami, OK. 74355

**Shawnee Tribe**
P.O. Box 222
Miami, OK. 74355

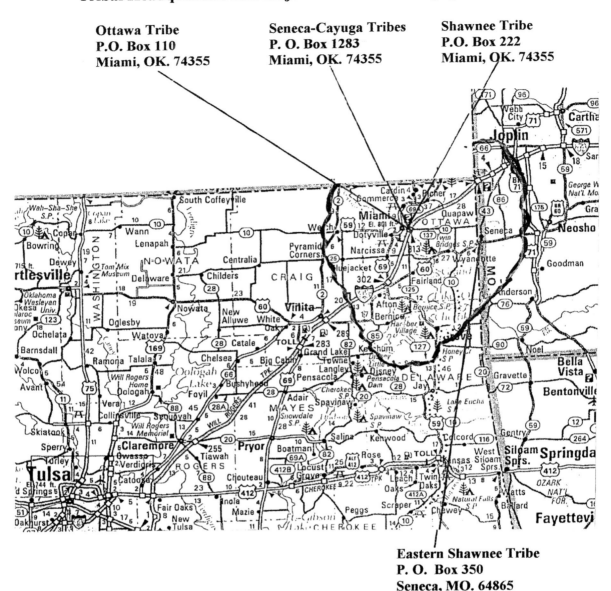

**Eastern Shawnee Tribe**
P. O. Box 350
Seneca, MO. 64865

## Notes on Sources

The People
There are many good works on the People that will help the reader expand their understanding of the People.

In regard to the Shawnee; the studies by R. David Edmunds, Carl Klinck, James Howard, and John Sugden are highly regarded.

The Seneca People's story is intertwined in the People of the Iroquois League, especially the Cayuga. The studies of Anthony Wallace, William Fenton, and R. David Edmunds will supplement the general histories.

The Ottawa People's story is intertwined with the Ojibwa and Pottawatomie in Michigan and the Wyandot in Ohio. The studies by W. Vernon Kinietz, the work of J. Clifton, C. Cornell, and J. McClurken, in a single volume are a starting point.

Setting the Stage
To understand the dynamics of the Ohio scene prior to removal, the studies of Colin Calloway, R. David Edmunds, Larry Nelson, Wiley Sword and Robert White head the list. Two other sources that should be used are The Newberry Libraries Atlas of Great Lakes Indian History, edited by Helen Hornbeck Tanner, and Erminie Wheeler-Voegelin's Indians of Northwest Ohio in the Garland American Indian Series. The removal period is sketched by several sources such as Grant Forman. The detailed study is done by Carl Klophenstein. To investigate the specific treaties: Commissioner of Indian Affairs (comp.), Treaties Between the United States of America and the Several Indian Tribes, from 1778 to 1837 (Washington, 1837); Charles J. Kappler (ed. and comp.), Indian Affairs, Laws and Treaties (4 vols., Washington, 1904-1929); Charles C. Royce (comp.), "Indian Land Cessions in the United States," in Eighteenth Annual Report of the Bureau of American Ethnology to the Secretary of the Smithsonian Institution, 1696-1897 (2 vols., Washington, 1899); and Correspondences on the Subject of the Emigration of Indians, in Senate Documents, 23 Cong., 1 Sess., No. 51265 vols., Nos. 244-246).

A Sorrowful Journey
Besides the government sources given in chapter 2, the following newspapers present some insight: Niles Weekly Register, 1832; Cincinnati Advertiser and Ohio Phoenix, 1831-1832; Cincinnati Liberty Hall and Cincinnati Gazette, 1831-1833; Ohio State Gazette, 1831; Ohio Sentinel, 1832; Ohio State Journal and Columbus Gazette, 1832-1833; Dayton Journal and Advertiser, 1829-1831; Hamilton Intelligencer, 1831-1833; Lebanon The Western Star, 1831-1833; Piqua Gazette, 1832-1833; and Piqua Gazette and Miami Farmers' General Intelligencer, 1831.

Two books to read to broaden the outlook on the events are: Henry Harvey, History of the Shawnee Indians, from the year 1681 to 1854, Inclusive (Cincinnati, 1855), and C. William, History of Western Ohio and Auglaize County with illustrations and biographical sketches of pioneers and pertinent public men (Columbus, 1904).

The writing of Daniel R. Dunihue in the government documents sited, "Dunihue Correspondence of 1832, Removal of Indians from Ohio," Indiana Magazine of History, XXXV (1939), pp.233-330, and "Dunihue Diary" online at http://www.connerpraire.org/decdiary.html.

The major source used as a base and starting point is the unpublished journal of John C. Shelby in a private collection.

If the reader wants to pursue the overall removal story; Helen Hunt Jackson, "A Century of Dishonor," Grant Forman, "The Last Trek of the Indians," Reginald Horsman, "The Origin of Indian Removal," and the works of Angie Bebo and Theda Perdue are a starting point.

# Index